WooCommerce Cookbook

Create, design, and manage your own personalized online store with WooCommerce, the fastest growing e-commerce platform

Patrick Rauland

[PACKT] **open source**✳
PUBLISHING   community experience distilled

BIRMINGHAM - MUMBAI

WooCommerce Cookbook

First published: March 2015

Production reference: 1240315

Published by Packt Publishing Ltd.
Livery Place
35 Livery Street
Birmingham B3 2PB, UK.

ISBN 978-1-78439-405-9

www.packtpub.com

Credits

Author

Patrick Rauland

Reviewers

Matthew Allan

Matt Cohen

Nicola Mustone

Commissioning Editor

Amit Ghodke

Acquisition Editor

Neha Nagwekar

Content Development Editor

Merwyn D'souza

Technical Editor

Rahul C. Shah

Copy Editors

Aditya Nair

Deepa Nambiar

Rashmi Sawant

Project Coordinator

Neha Bhatnagar

Proofreaders

Simran Bhogal

Stephen Copestake

Indexer

Rekha Nair

Production Coordinator

Alwin Roy

Cover Work

Alwin Roy

About the Author

Patrick Rauland has built custom e-commerce solutions as well as high-end WooCommerce sites while working for advertising agencies. He joined the support team at WooThemes and answered thousands of support tickets. He later joined the WooThemes development team and started writing the underlying code for WooCommerce. After several months on the development team, he took on the role of product manager, and interacts with customers and the development team to help plan the future of WooCommerce.

Patrick loves going to conferences to talk about e-commerce, software development, productivity, happiness, and creating your online presence.

Patrick lives in Denver, Colorado, and loves running, yoga, and hiking.

You can reach Patrick through his programming blog at `http://speakinginbytes.com`.

I couldn't have done anything worthwhile in my life, let alone write a book, without being inspired by so many people. The first person I have to mention is my friend Gerry Hazen. He spent hours listening to me blather about the latest book or blog post I just read. When I actually stumbled onto a good idea, he helped me refine the idea and follow through.

I also had a lot of inspiration from several people in the web industry. I look up to Brent Shepherd because he produces some of the highest quality software on the market. I look up to Daniel Espinoza because of his amazing grit when it comes to running his business to provide for his family; Matt Cohen for being able to refine any idea into its core components; and Michael Krapf for his big picture thinking and for taking a chance on me.

I want to thank my family for trusting that I'd find my way and for giving me the financial freedom to try all of these crazy ideas. Lastly, I want to thank Kristie Wirth, my partner, who hears all of the crazy ideas and helps me focus on one idea at a time.

About the Reviewers

Matthew Allan has exhibited a keen interest in business and e-commerce ever since he can remember. Over the past 3 years, he has been developing new software for entrepreneurs, wanting to jump into the e-commerce world and start selling online. Matthew's main focus since completing his degree in information technology has been on WordPress and WooCommerce extension development and support.

Matthew works with a small team of developers at Prospress Inc. to bring top-notch plugins and extensions to the WordPress and WooCommerce platforms. Some of Prospress' most well-known extensions are WooCommerce Subscriptions and WooCommerce One Page Checkout—both mentioned in the book and available from WooThemes.com.

Matthew's background in developing and supporting premium extensions for WooCommerce helped his technical review for this book.

Matt Cohen is the Chief Product Officer at WooThemes, a market leader in premium WordPress products, and the creators of WooCommerce. He spends his day managing his engineering team and a growing team of product managers.

With a deep love of web development, Matt began tinkering with HTML4 during high school (before CSS existed), which formed a strong bond with early web development languages and principles. Continuing his career, he worked as a senior developer at a handful of agencies prior to joining WooThemes as a senior web developer in late 2010. A love of product creation, customer experience, and well-architected products lead him to move into the Chief Product Officer role, where he oversees the design and creation of all products developed within WooThemes.

He has deep love for WordPress and is an engineer at his core, with a strong love of creating amazing customer experiences. In his personal time, he enjoys nature, punk rock, and forgotten 90s television.

Nicola Mustone is a web developer based in Italy, where he studied economics and programming. He developed his first website at the age of 15. From then, he fell in love with programming and web development, so he started studying it in depth, improving his skillset.

He started working as a freelancer at the age of 19. In 2011, he accepted his first job at a local web agency.

In 2012, Nicola moved from his birth city, Lucera, to Acireale in Sicily, to work with Your Inspiration where he learned about WordPress in its entirety, from end user usage to theme and plugin development. While working at Your Inspiration, he specialized in WordPress development and customer support.

In October 2014, he started working for WooThemes where he works and rocks out as a WooCommerce Support Ninja. Nicola also regularly writes articles and tutorials to help customers better understand WooCommerce and WordPress. You can reach him through his blog at `http://nicolamustone.it`.

www.PacktPub.com

Support files, eBooks, discount offers, and more

For support files and downloads related to your book, please visit www.PacktPub.com.

Did you know that Packt offers eBook versions of every book published, with PDF and ePub files available? You can upgrade to the eBook version at www.PacktPub.com and as a print book customer, you are entitled to a discount on the eBook copy. Get in touch with us at service@packtpub.com for more details.

At www.PacktPub.com, you can also read a collection of free technical articles, sign up for a range of free newsletters and receive exclusive discounts and offers on Packt books and eBooks.

https://www2.packtpub.com/books/subscription/packtlib

Do you need instant solutions to your IT questions? PacktLib is Packt's online digital book library. Here, you can search, access, and read Packt's entire library of books.

Why Subscribe?

- ▸ Fully searchable across every book published by Packt
- ▸ Copy and paste, print, and bookmark content
- ▸ On demand and accessible via a web browser

Free Access for Packt account holders

If you have an account with Packt at www.PacktPub.com, you can use this to access PacktLib today and view 9 entirely free books. Simply use your login credentials for immediate access.

Table of Contents

Preface

Up until just a few years ago, building your own e-commerce site was remarkably difficult. You had to install complex software, host it yourself, and hope that, whenever you made a change, nothing broke. That's very different from where we are now.

WooCommerce was released in September 2011 and, since then, it's taken the e-commerce world by storm. As of 2015, there are nearly 400,000 sites that run WooCommerce; that is approximately 18 percent of all e-commerce sites on the Internet and bigger than every other competitor by a wide margin (source: BuiltWith.com).

Part of the success of WooCommerce is because it's built on top of the incredibly popular WordPress platform. With just a few clicks, you can install the WooCommerce plugin and turn your WordPress site into an online store. With over 300 official extensions to customize your store, you no longer need a developer. You can add thousands of free plugins and themes to customize the rest of your WordPress site and the options are nearly limitless.

There are hosting companies that only host WordPress sites, services that maintain your WordPress sites for you, and professional products that handle every aspect of your site from creating contact forms to image optimization. The list goes on. What you need to know is that WordPress is huge and still growing. As WordPress grows, so will WooCommerce.

WooCommerce isn't only built on top of WordPress. It's also built on top of the WooThemes brand. WooThemes was one of the first companies to start building commercial themes and plugins for WordPress, and over the years they've perfected their techniques and poured it all into WooCommerce. Having to swap your e-commerce software would be a nightmare. That's part of the reason that WooCommerce has taken off so fast. It's backed by one of the biggest brands in the entire WordPress space. People know that they won't disappear any time soon.

In short, you can rest easy. WooCommerce is built on top of both a growing platform and a trusted brand.

Let's get started building your e-commerce site.

What this book covers

Chapter 1, WooCommerce Basics, covers how to install the software and configure the basic settings.

Chapter 2, Adding Products, deals with adding simple products to the store, downloadable files to a product, images and image galleries to a product and, variable products to the store; this chapter also covers bulk-uploading products.

Chapter 3, Changing the Product Organization, covers configuring your store to show off your products, adding more products on the shop page, adding a search capability, adding social media, sorting products, and adding extra information to the shop page.

Chapter 4, Running a Membership Site, deals with creating subscription products, using members-only pricing, creating premium content, and creating a pricing table.

Chapter 5, Setting Up Shipping Methods, deals with configuring Free Shipping and Flat Rate Shipping, getting live shipping quotes, tracking shipments, and creating advanced tables of shipping rates.

Chapter 6, Getting Paid, covers how to configure payment gateways such as PayPal, Stripe, and Simplify Commerce. It also covers how to configure HTTPS and adding e-commerce tracking with Google Analytics.

Chapter 7, Modifying the Checkout Process, deals with configuring terms and conditions, adding customers to your newsletter, adding and removing checkout fields, adding a one-page checkout, and adding default options to the checkout.

Chapter 8, Managing Orders and Taxes, covers refunding orders, importing existing orders, configuring order numbers, exporting order information, and configuring taxes.

Chapter 9, WooCommerce Theming, deals with adding a cart to the menu, using WooCommerce hooks, overriding WooCommerce templates and WooCommerce CSS, and creating product slide shows.

Chapter 10, Exploring More with WooCommerce, deals with enabling reviews, creating and cloaking affiliate links, creating coupons, and sending follow-up e-mails.

What you need for this book

WooCommerce is a plugin for WordPress. This means you already need to have your own self-hosted WordPress site. You cannot use a service such as WordPress.com that hosts the site for you.

Many of the recipes in this book require only WooCommerce itself. Some of them ask you to download a plugin from WordPress.org. Anything on WordPress.org will be completely free. Some recipes will require premium WooCommerce extensions. The vast majority of these are available on WooThemes.com. These extensions may be necessary for something such as, billing someone on a monthly basis, but they are not necessary for the core functionality. You can build a store without any extensions. If you don't wish to purchase any, you can skip the recipes that require these.

If you are a developer and you wish to use a test site, that will be fine. There are only a couple of recipes in this book that need an actual live site, and this requirement is clearly flagged in the introduction to the recipe.

Who this book is for

This book is meant for people who are setting up their own stores as well as freelance developers and designers who build sites for clients. The beginning of each chapter is meant for everyone. As the chapter progresses, we add a bit more complexity. I finished most chapters with code samples to show developers what they can do with a bit of code.

It helps if you already have experience with WordPress, but you don't need to be a WordPress expert by any means.

Sections

In this book, you will find several headings that appear frequently (Getting ready, How to do it, How it works, There's more, and See also).

To give clear instructions on how to complete a recipe, we use these sections as follows:

Getting ready

This section tells you what to expect in the recipe, and describes how to set up any software or any preliminary settings required for the recipe.

How to do it...

This section contains the steps required to follow the recipe.

How it works...

This section usually consists of a detailed explanation of what happened in the previous section.

There's more...

This section consists of additional information about the recipe in order to make the reader more knowledgeable about the recipe.

See also

This section provides helpful links to other useful information for the recipe.

Conventions

In this book, you will find a number of styles of text that distinguish between different kinds of information. Here are some examples of these styles, and an explanation of their meaning.

Code words in text, database table names, folder names, filenames, file extensions, pathnames, dummy URLs, user input, and Twitter handles are shown as follows: "We can include other contexts through the use of the `include` directive."

A block of code is set as follows:

```
function woocommerce_cookbook_subscription_intervals( $intervals )
{
    $intervals[10] = sprintf( __( 'every %s', 'my-text-domain' ),
WC_Subscriptions::append_numeral_suffix( 10 ) );
    return $intervals;
}
```

New terms and **important words** are shown in bold. Words that you see on the screen, in menus or dialog boxes for example, appear in the text like this: "clicking the **Next** button moves you to the next screen".

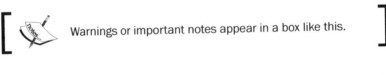

Warnings or important notes appear in a box like this.

Tips and tricks appear like this.

Reader feedback

Feedback from our readers is always welcome. Let us know what you think about this book—what you liked or may have disliked. Reader feedback is important for us to develop titles that you really get the most out of.

To send us general feedback, simply send an e-mail to feedback@packtpub.com, and mention the book title via the subject of your message. If there is a topic that you have expertise in and you are interested in either writing or contributing to a book, see our author guide on www.packtpub.com/authors.

Customer support

Now that you are the proud owner of a Packt book, we have a number of things to help you to get the most from your purchase.

Downloading the example code

You can download the example code files for all Packt books you have purchased from your account at http://www.packtpub.com. If you purchased this book elsewhere, you can visit http://www.packtpub.com/support and register to have the files e-mailed directly to you.

Errata

Although we have taken every care to ensure the accuracy of our content, mistakes do happen. If you find a mistake in one of our books—maybe a mistake in the text or the code—we would be grateful if you would report this to us. By doing so, you can save other readers from frustration and help us improve subsequent versions of this book. If you find any errata, please report them by visiting http://www.packtpub.com/submit-errata, selecting your book, clicking on the **errata submission form** link, and entering the details of your errata. Once your errata are verified, your submission will be accepted and the errata will be uploaded on our website, or added to any list of existing errata, under the Errata section of that title. Any existing errata can be viewed by selecting your title from http://www.packtpub.com/support.

Piracy

Piracy of copyright material on the Internet is an ongoing problem across all media. At Packt, we take the protection of our copyright and licenses very seriously. If you come across any illegal copies of our works, in any form, on the Internet, please provide us with the location address or website name immediately so that we can pursue a remedy.

Please contact us at `copyright@packtpub.com` with a link to the suspected pirated material.

We appreciate your help in protecting our authors, and our ability to bring you valuable content.

Questions

You can contact us at `questions@packtpub.com` if you are having a problem with any aspect of the book, and we will do our best to address it.

1
WooCommerce Basics

In this chapter, we will cover:

- ▶ Installing WooCommerce
- ▶ Setting your store location and currency
- ▶ Finding documentation on WooThemes.com
- ▶ Installing WooCommerce plugins
- ▶ Installing official WooThemes plugins
- ▶ Manually creating WooCommerce pages
- ▶ Creating a WooCommerce plugin
- ▶ Adding a currency to WooCommerce

Introduction

A few years ago, building an online store used to be an incredibly complex task. You had to install bulky software onto your own website and pay expensive developers a significant sum of money to customize even the simplest elements of your store. Luckily, nowadays, adding e-commerce functionality to your existing WordPress-powered website can be done by installing a single plugin. In this chapter, we'll go over the settings that you'll need to configure *before* launching your online store with WooCommerce. Most of the recipes in this chapter are simple to execute. We do, however, add a relatively complex recipe near the end of the chapter to show you how to create a plugin specifically for WooCommerce. If you're going to be customizing WooCommerce with code, it's definitely worth looking at that recipe to know the best way to customize WooCommerce without affecting other parts of your site.

The recipes in this chapter form the very basics of setting up a store, installing plugins that enhance WooCommerce, and managing those plugins. There are recipes for official WooCommerce plugins written using WooThemes as well as a recipe for unofficial plugins. Feel free to select either one. In general, the official plugins are better supported, more up to date, and have more functionality than unofficial plugins. You could always try an unofficial plugin to see whether it meets your needs, and if it doesn't, then use an official plugin that is much more likely to meet your needs.

At the end of this chapter, your store will be fully functional and ready to display products. In *Chapter 2, Adding Products*, we will learn how to add products to our store.

Installing WooCommerce

WooCommerce is a WordPress plugin, which means that you need to have WordPress running on your own server to add WooCommerce. The first step is to install WooCommerce. You could do this on an established website or a brand new website—it doesn't matter. Since e-commerce is more complex than your average plugin, there's more to the installation process than just installing the plugin.

Getting ready

Make sure you have the permissions necessary to install plugins on your WordPress site. The easiest way to have the correct permissions is to make sure your account on your WordPress site has the admin role.

How to do it...

There are two parts to this recipe. The first part is installing the plugin and the second step is adding the required pages to the site. Let's have a look at the following steps for further clarity:

1. Log in to your WordPress site.
2. Click on the **Plugins** menu.
3. Click on the **Add New** menu item. These steps have been demonstrated visually in the following screenshot:

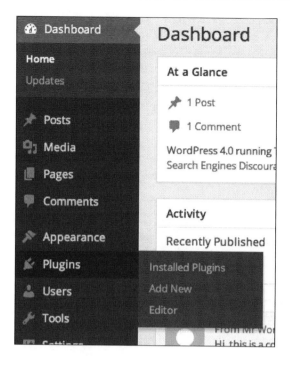

4. Search for WooCommerce.

5. Click on the **Install Now** button, as shown in the following screenshot:

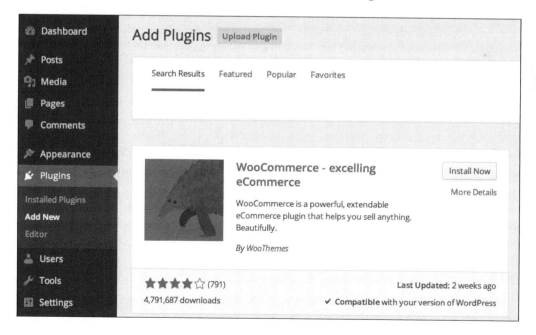

6. Once the plugin has been installed, click on the **Activate Plugin** button. You now have WooCommerce activated on your site, which means we're half way there. E-commerce platforms need to have certain pages (such as a cart page, a checkout page, an account page, and so on) to function. We need to add those to your site.

7. Click on the **Install WooCommerce Pages** button, which appears after you've activated WooCommerce. This is demonstrated in the following screenshot:

How it works...

WordPress has an infrastructure that allows any WordPress site to install a plugin hosted on WordPress.org. This is a secure process that is managed by WordPress.org.

Installing the WooCommerce pages allows all of the e-commerce functionality to run. Without installing the pages, WooCommerce won't know which page is the cart page or the checkout page. Once these pages are set up, we're ready to have a basic store up and running.

> If WordPress prompts you for FTP credentials when installing the plugin, that's likely to be a permissions issue with your web host. It is a huge pain if you have to enter FTP credentials every time you want to install or update a plugin, and it's something you should take care of. You can send this link to your web host provider so they know how to change their permissions. You can refer to `http://www.chrisabernethy.com/why-wordpress-asks-connection-info/` for more information to resolve this WordPress issue.

Setting your store location and currency

WooCommerce is an e-commerce platform that can work anywhere in the world. You can enable it to use any location or currency. WooCommerce was originally created by developers in the UK, so the default settings are all UK-based. If you don't live in the UK, you'll have to change your store location and currency.

Getting ready

You'll need a WordPress site with WooCommerce installed.

How to do it...

Since you're looking for ways to customize your store functionality, you can do a lot using the WooCommerce settings pages. Before looking through code or asking for a developer's help, it's worth looking through all of the settings pages to see whether any issue you have can be fixed right there. Changing the store location and currency can both be done on the settings pages with a couple of clicks, by performing the following steps:

1. Go to **WooCommerce | Settings**:

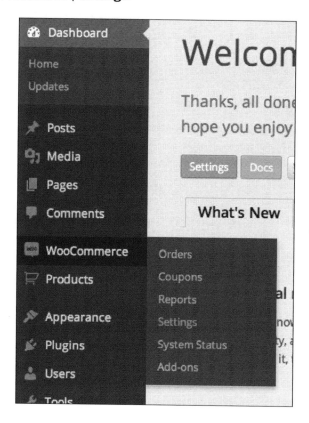

2. Click on the **Base Location** setting and start typing the name of your province or country. Many countries, such as the United States, have different provinces, so it's best to see whether your province is listed in **WooCommerce**. If it is, select the province; if not, select your country. Have a look at the following screenshot:

3. Scroll down to the **Currency Options** section.

4. From the **Currency** dropdown, select your currency.

How it works...

WooCommerce has a huge list of countries and currencies built in. You can select the right one on the **Settings** screen and WooCommerce will save this information in the database and use it for shipping, taxes, and other purposes. You can programmatically add more countries and currencies to WooCommerce, and those updated lists will show up on the settings pages.

If your currency doesn't appear in the list, it can be manually added. You may also refer to the *Adding a currency to WooCommerce* recipe at the end of this chapter.

Finding documentation on WooThemes.com

WooCommerce has been developed by WooThemes, a WordPress theme and plugin development shop. In addition to developing the plugin, they've also created hundreds of pages of documentation for WooCommerce and all of the extensions.

If you want to dig into exactly what settings are available and how they interact with other settings, you should know how to find the documentation in the first place. Some people like to read through the documentation ahead of time and others like to explore the settings without reading the documentation and only refer to it if they are stuck. Either way works.

How to do it...

The documentation can be accessed directly via the WooThemes website. It can also be accessed from your WordPress site. Follow these steps to find the documentation:

1. In the WordPress admin, click on the **Plugins** menu to see the list of installed plugins.

2. Click on the **Docs** link under **WooCommerce**, as shown in the following screenshot, which will take you to the documentation on `http://www.woothemes.com`:

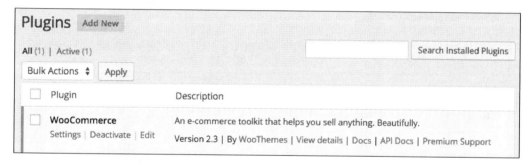

3. Now that you're in the documentation section, navigate to the section you need. **Getting Started** is great for someone just starting their store, **Codex** is great for people who want to customize **WooCommerce** or their theme, and **Extensions** is great for any WooCommerce extensions you may have.

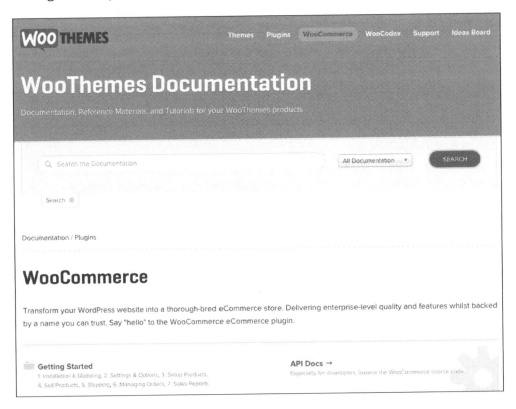

Installing WooCommerce plugins

WooCommerce is open source and free, which means that any developer can add extra functionality to WooCommerce. Some developers may add this extra functionality with a WordPress plugin and then release the plugin either for free or as a premium plugin.

There are three likely places to get a WooCommerce plugin: from WooThemes, from WordPress.org, or from a third-party website. In this recipe, we'll be installing a plugin obtained from a third-party site. Installing a WooCommerce plugin from WordPress.org is similar to installing WooCommerce. We will have a look at how to install official WooThemes plugins in the next recipe.

Getting ready

Make sure you have the necessary permissions to install plugins on your WordPress site and that you have WooCommerce installed.

How to do it...

We're going to be downloading a plugin I created as an example of how to create an extra WooCommerce settings page, by performing the following steps:

1. Go to `https://gist.github.com/BFTrick/b5e3afa6f4f83ba2e54a/`.
2. Click on **Download Gist**.

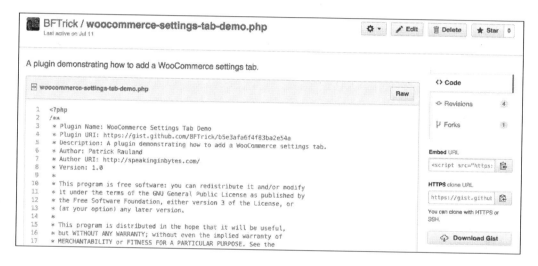

3. Make sure your plugin is in the `.zip` format. By looking at the downloaded file, we can see that our file ends in `.tar.gz`, which is not the right format:

We need to convert this to the `.zip` format. Here's what you need to do on a Mac operating system:

1. Double-click on the `.tar.gz` file, which will create a new folder.

2. Right-click on the new folder and click on **Compress gistb5e3afa6f4f83ba2...9**.

And this is what you need to do on a Windows operating system:

3. Windows cannot extract a `.tar.gz` file natively. You'll have to install a software to do so. A free tool is 7-Zip, which can be found at `http://www.7-zip.org/`.

4. In your WordPress admin, click on the **Plugins** menu and then on **Add New**:

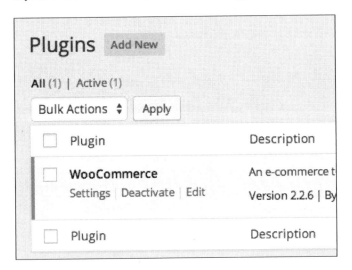

5. Click on **Upload Plugin**:

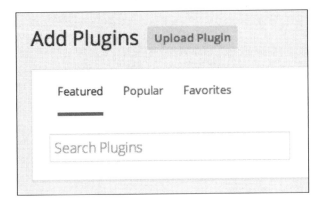

6. On the new screen, choose the zipped file to be uploaded and click on **Install Now**.

7. Once the plugin has finished installing, click on the **Activate Plugin** link. The following screen should appear:

Installing Plugin from uploaded file: gistb5e3afa6f4f83ba2e54a-bb6dc1e76c9aee652bc2cd0925803b1df1cf3da9.zip

Unpacking the package…

Installing the plugin…

Plugin installed successfully.

Activate Plugin | Return to Plugins page

You now have a WooCommerce plugin installed on your site. If you want to see what this plugin does, you can navigate to the WooCommerce settings page and click on **Settings Demo Tab**.

How it works...

WordPress can import any ZIP file. As long as the plugin was created correctly, WordPress shouldn't have any problems running the plugin. If there is a problem, WordPress will let you know that the plugin has invalid code.

Installing official WooThemes plugins

WooThemes doesn't just create the WooCommerce plugin. They also create standalone plugins and hundreds of extensions that add extra functionality to WooCommerce. The beauty of this system is that WooCommerce is very easy to use because users only add extra complexity when they need it. If you only need simple shipping options, you don't ever have to see the complex shipping settings.

On the WooThemes website, you may browse for WooCommerce extensions, purchase them, and download and install them on your site. WooThemes has made the whole process very easy to maintain. They have built an updater similar to the one in WordPress, which, once configured, will allow a user to update a plugin with one click instead of having to through the whole plugin upload process again.

Getting ready

Make sure you have the necessary permissions to install plugins on your WordPress site. You also need to have a WooThemes product. There are several free WooThemes products including Pay with Amazon which you can find at `http://www.woothemes.com/products/pay-with-amazon/`.

How to do it...

There are two parts to this recipe. The first part is installing the plugin and the second step is adding your license for future updates. Follow these steps:

1. Log in to `http://www.woothemes.com`.

2. Click on the **Downloads** menu:

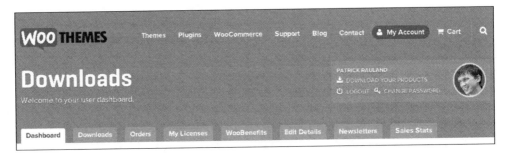

3. Find the product you wish to download and click on the **Download** link for the product. You will see that you get a ZIP file.

4. On your WordPress site, go the **Plugins** menu and click on **Add New**.

5. Click on **Upload Plugin**.

6. Select the file you just downloaded and click on the **Install Now** button.

7. After the plugin has finished installing, click on the **Activate Plugin** link.

You now have WooCommerce as well as a WooCommerce extension activated on your site. They're both functioning and will continue to function. You will, however, want to perform a few more steps to make sure it's easy to update your extensions:

1. Once you have an extension activated on your site, you'll see a link in the WordPress admin: **Install the WooThemes Updater plugin**. Click on that link:

2. The updater will be installed automatically.

3. Once it is installed, you need to activate the updater.

4. After activation, you'll see a new link in the WordPress admin: **activate your product licenses**. Click that link to go straight to the page where you can enter your licenses. You could also navigate to that page manually by going to **Dashboard | WooThemes Helper** from the menu.

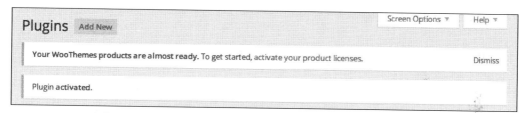

5. Keep your WordPress site open in one tab and log back in to your WooThemes account in another browser tab.

6. On the WooThemes browser tab, go to **My Licenses** and you'll see a list of your products with a license key under the heading **KEY**:

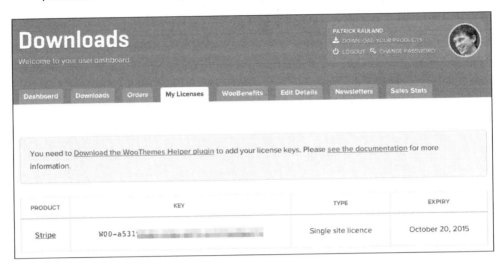

7. Copy the key, go back to your WordPress site, and enter it in the **Licenses** field.

8. Click on the **Activate Products** button at the bottom of the page. The activation process can take a few seconds to complete.

9. If you've successfully put in your key, you should see a message at the top of the screen saying so.

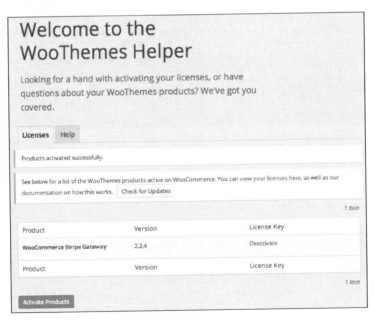

How it works...

A plugin that's not hosted on WordPress.org can't update without someone manually reuploading it. The WooThemes updater was built to make this process easier so you can press the **update** button and have your website do all the heavy lifting.

Some websites sell official WooCommerce plugins without a license key. These sales aren't licensed and you won't be getting updates, bug fixes, or access to the support desk. With a regular website, it's important to stay up to date. However, with e-commerce, it's even more important since you'll be handling very sensitive payment information. That's why I wouldn't ever recommend using a plugin that can't update.

Refer to the preceding recipe, *Installing WooCommerce plugins*, for more details. There are several screenshots in that recipe about the general process of uploading a WordPress plugin.

Manually creating WooCommerce pages

Every e-commerce platform will need to have some way of creating extra pages for e-commerce functionality, such as a cart page, a checkout page, an account page, and so on. WooCommerce prompts to helps you create these pages for you when you first install the plugin. So if you installed it correctly, you shouldn't have to do this. But if you were trying multiple e-commerce systems and for some reason deleted some pages, you may have to recreate those pages.

How to do it...

There's a very useful **Tools** menu in WooCommerce. It's a bit hard to find since you won't be needing it everyday, but it has some pretty useful tools if you ever need to do some troubleshooting. One of these tools is the one that allows you to recreate your WooCommerce pages. Let's have a look at how to use that tool:

1. Log in to the WordPress admin.

2. Click on **WooCommerce | System Status**:

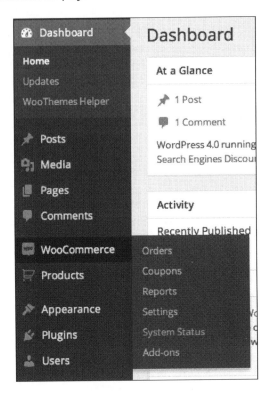

3. Click on **Tools**:

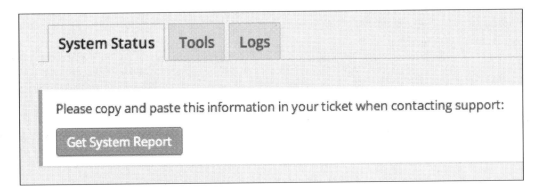

4. Click on the **Install Pages** button:

System Status	Tools	Logs

Tools

WC Transients	Clear transients	This tool will clear the product/shop transients cache.
Expired Transients	Clear expired transients	This tool will clear ALL expired transients from WordPress.
Term counts	Recount terms	This tool will recount product terms - useful when changing your settings in a way which hides products from the catalog.
Capabilities	Reset capabilities	This tool will reset the admin, customer and shop_manager roles to default. Use this if your users cannot access all of the WooCommerce admin pages.
Customer Sessions	Clear all sessions	Warning: This tool will delete all customer session data from the database, including any current live carts.
Install WooCommerce Pages	Install pages	Note: This tool will install all the missing WooCommerce pages. Pages already defined and set up will not be replaced.

How it works...

WooCommerce keeps track of which pages run e-commerce functionality. When you click on the **Install Pages** button, it checks which pages exist and if they don't exist, it will automatically create them for you. You could create them by creating new WordPress pages and then manually assigning each page with specific e-commerce functionality. You may want to do this if you already have a cart page and don't want to recreate a new cart page but just copy the content from the old page to the new page. All you want to do is tell WooCommerce which page should have the cart functionality. Let's have a look at the following manual settings:

- The **Cart**, **Checkout**, and **Terms & Conditions** page can all be set by going to **WooCommerce | Settings | Checkout**
- The **My Account** page can be set by going to **WooCommerce | Settings | Accounts**

There's more...

You can manually set some pages, such as the **Cart** and **Checkout** page, but you can't set subpages. WooCommerce uses a WordPress functionality called **end points** to create these subpages. Pages such as the **Order Received** page, which is displayed right after payment, can't be manually created. These endpoints are created on the fly based on the parent page. The **Order Received** page is part of the checkout process, so it's based on the **Checkout** page. Any content on the **Checkout** page will appear on both the **Checkout** page and on the **Order Received** page.

You can't add content to the parent page without it affecting the subpage, but you can change the subpage URLs. The checkout endpoints can be configured by going to **WooCommerce | Settings | Checkout | Checkout Endpoints**.

Creating a WooCommerce plugin

Unlike a lot of hosted e-commerce solutions, WooCommerce is entirely customizable. That's one of the huge advantages for anyone who builds on open source software. If you don't like it, you can change it. At some point, you'll probably want to change something that's not on a settings page, and that's when you may want to dig into the code. Even if you don't know how to code, you may want to look this over so that when you work with a developer, you would know they're doing it the right way.

Getting ready

In addition to having admin access to a WordPress site, you'll also need FTP credentials so you can upload a plugin. You'll also need a text editor. Popular code editors include Sublime Text, Coda, Dreamweaver, and Atom. I personally use Atom. You could also use Notepad on a Windows machine or Text Edit on a Mac in a pinch.

How to do it...

We're going to be creating a plugin that interacts with WooCommerce. It will take the existing WooCommerce functionality and change it. These are the WooCommerce basics. If you build a plugin like this correctly, when WooCommerce isn't active, it won't do anything at all and won't slow down your website. Let's create a plugin by performing the following steps:

1. Open your text editor and create a new file. Save the file as `woocommerce-demo-plugin.php`.
2. In that file, add the opening PHP tag, which looks like this: `<?php`.

3. On the next line, add a plugin header. This allows WordPress to recognize the file as a plugin so that it can be activated. It looks something like the following:

```
/**
 * Plugin Name: WooCommerce Demo Plugin
 * Plugin URI: https://gist.github.com/
BFTrick/3ab411e7cec43eff9769
 * Description: A WooCommerce demo plugin
 * Author: Patrick Rauland
 * Author URI: http://speakinginbytes.com/
 * Version: 1.0
 *
 * This program is free software: you can redistribute it and/or
modify
 * it under the terms of the GNU General Public License as
published by
 * the Free Software Foundation, either version 3 of the License,
or
 * (at your option) any later version.
 *
 * This program is distributed in the hope that it will be useful,
 * but WITHOUT ANY WARRANTY; without even the implied warranty of
 * MERCHANTABILITY or FITNESS FOR A PARTICULAR PURPOSE. See the
 * GNU General Public License for more details.
 *
 * You should have received a copy of the GNU General Public
License
 * along with this program. If not, see <http://www.gnu.org/
licenses/>.
 *
 */
```

4. Now that WordPress knows that your file is a plugin, it's time to add some functionality to this. The first thing a good developer does is makes sure their plugin won't conflict with another plugin. To do that, we make sure an existing class doesn't have the same name as our class. I'll be using the `WC_Demo_Plugin` class, but you can use any class name you want. Add the following code beneath the plugin header:

```
if ( class_exists( 'WC_Demo_Plugin' ) ) {
    return;
}

class WC_Demo_Plugin {

}
```

5. Our class doesn't do anything yet, but at least we've written it in such a way that it won't break another plugin. There's another good practice we should add to our plugin before we add the functionality, and that's some logic to make sure another plugin won't misuse our plugin. In the vast majority of use cases, you want to make sure there can't be two instances of your code running. In computer science, this is called the **Singleton pattern**. This can be controlled by tracking the instances of the plugin with a variable. Right after the `WC_Demo_Plugin {` line, add the following:

```
protected static $instance = null;
```

```
/**
 * Return an instance of this class.
 *
 * @return object A single instance of this class.
 * @since   1.0
 */
public static function get_instance() {
    // If the single instance hasn't been set, set it now.
    if ( null == self::$instance ) {
        self::$instance = new self;
    }

    return self::$instance;
}
```

And get the plugin started by adding this right before the `endif;` line:

```
add_action( 'plugins_loaded', array( 'WC_Demo_Plugin',
'get_instance' ), 0 );
```

6. At this point, we've made sure our plugin doesn't break other plugins and we've also dummy-proofed our own plugin so that we or other developers don't misuse it. Let's add just a bit more logic so that we don't run our logic unless WooCommerce is already loaded. This will make sure that we don't accidentally break something if we turn WooCommerce off temporarily. Right after the `protected static $instance = null;` line, add the following:

```
/**
 * Initialize the plugin.
 *
 * @since 1.0
 */
private function __construct() {
```

```
            if ( class_exists( 'WooCommerce' ) ) {

        }
    }
```

7. And now our plugin only runs when WooCommerce is loaded. I'm guessing that at this point, you finally want it to do something, right? After we make sure WooCommerce is running, let's add some functionality. Right after the `if ( class_exists( 'WooCommerce' ) ) {` line, add the following code so that we add an admin notice:

```
// print an admin notice to the screen.
add_action( 'admin_notices', array( $this,
'my_admin_notice' ) );
```

This code will call a method called `my_admin_notice`, but we haven't written that yet, so it's not doing anything. Let's write that method. Have a look at the __construct method, which should now look like this:

```
/**
 * Initialize the plugin.
 *
 * @since 1.0
 */
private function __construct() {
    if ( class_exists( 'WooCommerce' ) ) {

        // print an admin notice to the screen.
        add_action( 'admin_notices', array( $this, 'display_admin_
notice' ) );

    }
}
```

Add the following after the preceding __construct method:

```
/**
 * Print an admin notice
 *
 * @since 1.0
 */
public function display_admin_notice() {
    ?>
    <div class="updated">
```

```
        <p><?php _e( 'The WooCommerce dummy plugin notice.',
'woocommerce-demo-plugin' ); ?></p>
    </div>
    <?php
}
```

This will print an admin notice on every single admin page. This notice includes all the messages you typically see in the WordPress admin. You could replace this admin notice method with just about any other hook in WooCommerce to provide additional customizations in other areas of WooCommerce, whether it be for shipping, the product page, the checkout process, or any other area. This plugin is the easiest way to get started with WooCommerce customizations.

> If you'd like to see the full code sample, you can see it at `https://gist.github.com/BFTrick/3ab411e7cec43eff9769`.

8. Now that the plugin is complete, you need to upload it to your `plugins` folder. You can do this via the WordPress admin or more commonly via FTP.

9. Once the plugin has been uploaded to your site, you'll need to activate the plugin just like any other WordPress plugin. The end result is a notice in the WordPress admin letting us know we did everything successfully.

STEVEN POTTSCHMIDT

Whenever possible, use object-oriented code. That means using objects (like the `WC_Demo_Plugin` class) to encapsulate your code. It will prevent a lot of naming conflicts down the road. If you see some procedural code online, you can usually convert it to object-oriented code pretty easily. Object-oriented programming is out of the scope of this book, but you can read more at `http://codex.wordpress.org/Plugin_API`.

Adding a currency to WooCommerce

WooCommerce has dozens of currencies already included in the plugin, including but not limited to US dollars, euros, British pounds, New Zealand dollars, Russian rubles, South African rands, Egyptian pounds, and the Mexican peso. If you are planning on using any of these currencies, you don't need to add your own currency and can skip this recipe. If you can't find your currency under **WooCommerce | Settings | Currency**, then you should follow the steps that follow to add it in.

Getting ready

We'll be writing some code to add your custom currency. You'll need a text editor to write the code and an FTP program to upload it to your site once we're done.

How to do it...

We're going to write a very small snippet and add it to WooCommerce. Once it's added, we'll select the currency from the **Currency** dropdown in the WooCommerce settings pages. The following are the steps that illustrate the process of creating custom currencies:

1. Open up your theme's `functions.php` file, located at `wp-content/themes/your-theme-name/functions.php`, with your text editor.

2. At the bottom of the file, we'll need to add two filters to add this currency to WooCommerce. These filters will accept an array with the existing currencies and add another option to the array. The first filter will add the currency to WooCommerce. The second will add the currency symbol. Have a look at the code for these filters:

```
add_filter( 'woocommerce_currencies',
'add_patricks_currency' );
add_filter( 'woocommerce_currency_symbol',
'add_patricks_currency_symbol', 10, 2 );
```

3. Now let's write the first one, which adds the currency itself. You'll need the name of the currency, which you can append in place of the term `Patrick&#39;s Currency` in the snippet that follows. You'll also need the three-character ISO code of the currency, which can be found at `http://en.wikipedia.org/wiki/ISO_4217`. This can replace `PC` in the following code snippet:

```
function add_patricks_currency( $currencies ) {
    $currencies['PC'] = __( 'Patrick&#39;s Currency',
'your-theme-name' );
    return $currencies;
}
```

4. We're halfway there. Now we need to add the currency symbol. You'll obviously need the currency symbol, which you can use to replace the dollar sign in the snippet that follows. You'll need to use the same currency ISO code you used in the preceding snippet. Let's have a look at the code:

```
function add_patricks_currency_symbol( $currency_symbol,
$currency ) {
    switch( $currency ) {
        case 'PC': $currency_symbol = 'PC'; break;
    }
    return $currency_symbol;
}
```

At this point, WooCommerce should know both your currency and your currency symbol, so it's worth uploading it and making sure we did it right. Upload the file via FTP.

Navigate to the **Currency** settings by going to **WooCommerce | Settings**. You should see your new currency in the **Currency** dropdown:

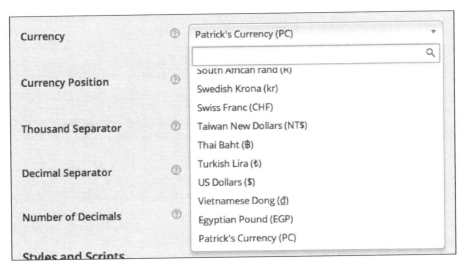

How it works...

WooCommerce is filled with hooks—places where developers can add or modify the existing code. WooCommerce was smartly built so that anyone can use these hooks to add (or remove) any number of currencies. In this case, we used a filter which is a special type of hook to change the value of something. We changed the contents in an array.

In future recipes, we'll be using **actions**, which allow completely new programming to fire, and not just changing the value of something.

See also

- We added this snippet to the theme's `functions.php` file. That works, but it's not as bulletproof as putting it in its own WooCommerce plugin. Refer to the preceding recipe, *Creating a WooCommerce plugin*, for more details.

2
Adding Products

In this chapter, we will cover:

- ▸ Adding a simple product
- ▸ Adding an image gallery to a product
- ▸ Changing image sizes in WooCommerce
- ▸ Adding a downloadable file to a product
- ▸ Adding global product attributes
- ▸ Adding a variable product
- ▸ Adding an extra fee to a product with the Product Add-ons plugin
- ▸ Adding a product bundle with the Product Bundles plugin
- ▸ Bulk-uploading products with a CSV file
- ▸ Removing product tabs
- ▸ Reordering product tabs

Introduction

In *Chapter 1, WooCommerce Basics*, you set up your store. The recipes in this chapter are all about adding products to your store. There are many different ways to configure your products. Knowing a little bit about each will help you decide how you want to display your products to your customer. Near the end of the chapter, we'll also touch on removing or reorganizing some of the information on the product page.

WooCommerce started with just simple and variable products. Over the years, other developers have come in and created different ways to sell products. In this chapter, we'll look at simple products, variable products, the **Product Add-ons** plugin, and the **Product Bundles** plugin. There are other ways to configure your products, but these are some of the most commonly used ones. At the end of this chapter, you should have all of the products in your store configured the way you want them. In *Chapter 3, Changing the Product Organization,* we'll cover how to manipulate the product page that the customer sees.

Adding a simple product

The best place to start when learning how you can add products to WooCommerce is to add a simple product. A simple product is the most basic product that you can create in WooCommerce. All other product types are based on the simple product and add extra controls.

How to do it...

In order to add a simple product to WooCommerce, take a look at the following steps:

1. Go to **Products | Add Product**.

2. Enter the name of the product in the **Product name** field. In the text editor right beneath the **Product name** field, enter the product's description. In most themes, this copy will appear beneath the product, so you could write paragraphs and paragraphs if you wish.

3. Scroll down to the **Product Data** panel.

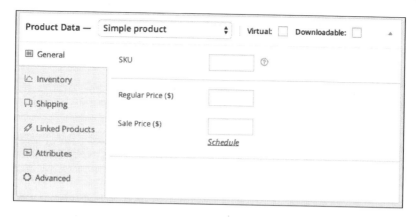

4. Enter the product's price in the **Regular Price ($)** field.

5. Scroll down to the **Product Short Description** panel and enter a short description of the product. This copy will appear above the **Buy** button, so it's best if it's only one or two lines. It is usually a summary of the full description.

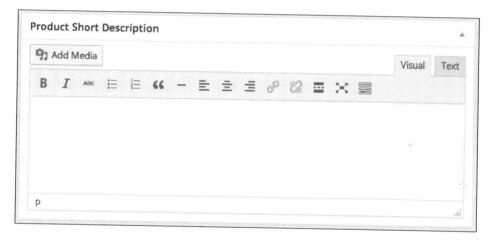

6. Look for the **Featured Image** panel in the sidebar. Click on **Set featured image** and then, in the pop-up that appears, either pick an existing image or upload an image.

7. Click on the **Publish** button.

This is, of course, just the tip of the iceberg. It is the bare minimum amount of information necessary to sell a product.

If you're already comfortable with WordPress and how categories and tags work, you could add those to your product at this point.

In subsequent recipes, we'll add even more information to your products.

Adding an image gallery to a product

One of the things that can really sell a product is having high-quality visuals. For some types of products, you may only need one photo. For other markets, especially upper-scale markets, the more photos, the better. Included in WooCommerce is the ability to show off a gallery of images.

Getting ready

You need to have a product on your site. If you haven't already done this, please follow the steps in the preceding recipe, *Adding a simple product*.

How to do it...

In order to add an image gallery to a product, go through the following steps:

1. In the WordPress admin, click on the **Products** menu and navigate to your product.

2. Once you're on the product detail page, look for the **Product Gallery** meta box and click on **Add product gallery images**.

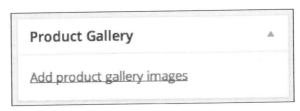

3. Just like with the **Featured Image** configuration, you can either select existing images or upload as many images as you like.

4. Now that you've added the images to the product gallery, you can arrange them however you like by clicking-and-dragging them into any order.

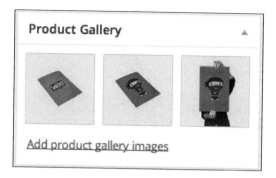

5. Click on **Update** and you should have a beautiful gallery for your product.

 Included in WooCommerce is a **lightbox gallery**. If you click on any of the images in the gallery, it should open the image up in a lightbox. Make sure you upload high-quality images as the lightbox will display the largest size available.

Changing image sizes in WooCommerce

If your products fit nicely into perfectly square images and they look good as they are in your theme, then you can probably skip this recipe. For some themes or some types of products, though, it's really beneficial to change how WooCommerce crops your images. If you're selling ties, for example, it's probably worth telling WooCommerce to crop them so they're long and skinny.

Getting ready

It's best if you have already created a couple of products and look at them to compare how the **Featured Image** and the **Product Gallery** look on their product pages. If you see gaps around the images, you may be able to increase the product image size and take advantage of that space.

How to do it...

Changing image sizes can be done in two parts. The first part will change the settings, and this will affect all future uploads. The second part will install a plugin that will force your website to recrop every image, which will affect all past uploads. Let's have a look at the following steps that depict these two parts:

1. From the WordPress admin, go to **WooCommerce | Settings**.
2. Click on the **Products** tab.
3. Click on the **Display** tab and then scroll down to **Product Image Sizes**.

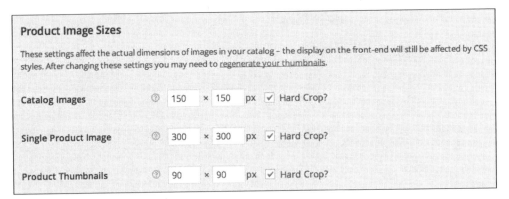

4. Enter your new sizes.
5. **Catalog Images** controls the size on the shop page and category pages.

6. **Single Product Image** controls the size of the featured image on the product page.

7. **Product Thumbnails** controls the size of the gallery thumbnails on the product page.

8. When you're done, click on the **Save changes** button at the bottom of the page.

Now that you have the new images set, any future uploads will use those settings. We'll have to install a free plugin to resize all of the existing images. Let's have a look at the following steps that illustrate the step-by-step installation of this plugin:

1. Add a new plugin under **Plugins | Add New**.

2. Run a search for, and install and activate, the **Regenerate Thumbnails** plugin.

3. Click on **Tools | Regen. Thumbnails**.

4. Click on **Regenerate All Thumbnails** and wait for your site to process all of the images.

You should now be able to go back to any of your product pages and see the new image size. In my case, I made the main featured image tall and skinny by setting **Single Product Image** to 150 x 300.

We are now done with changing the image sizes for your products.

 You might be able to see a little bit of distortion in my image. That's because I uploaded an image that's too small. WooCommerce blew it up to fit the dimensions I specified. If you don't want to have blurry images, the best piece of advice is to upload high-quality large images. You can also follow this video tutorial at `http://docs.woothemes.com/document/using-the-appropriate-product-image-dimensions/`. If you want to learn more about the different ways you can crop images and what the different types of cropping are, there is a great article on WPExplorer at `http://www.wpexplorer.com/wordpress-image-crop-sizes/`.

Adding a downloadable file to a product

WooCommerce is just as good to sell **virtual products** as it is to sell physical products. The beauty of the way it's set up is that any product type can be a virtual product. It could be a **simple product**, a **variable product**, a **subscription product** (which we'll cover in *Chapter 4, Running a Membership Site*), and so on. WooCommerce handles all of the download permissions. Fulfilling virtual products is completely automated. As soon as you receive payment, the customer receives an email with a special link to download to the file.

The simple product I set up in previous recipes is a poster. I could change this product so that it includes a digital download in addition to the physical product or I could even change it so that the customer only receives a digital download and there is no physical product shipped.

Getting ready

Make sure you already have a simple product in your store.

How to do it...

In the first section, I'm going to add a downloadable file to a product. The customer will receive the download immediately and the physical product after it's shipped. In the second section, we'll show you how to make the product only sell a downloadable file and skip the whole shipping process. Let's have a look at the following steps:

1. In the WordPress admin, click on the **Products** menu and navigate to your product.
2. Under the **Product Data** panel, you'll see a **Downloadable** checkbox. Check it.

3. Under **Downloadable Files**, click on the **Add File** button. You can add as many downloadable files as you wish.

4. The **File URL** will automatically be filled in. You can now enter a friendly name for the file that the user will see. This could be something like woo-poster.

At this point, you can fill in the additional download settings. This is purely optional. Some store owners like to lock down the downloads, preventing them from being downloaded too many times.

If you have a product that's purely virtual and doesn't ship any physical component, there's a little bit more we should do.

5.   On the **Product Data** panel, check the **Virtual** checkbox.

Now your product will skip the shipping process altogether. Note that the shipping tab on the **Product Data** panel has disappeared since there are no shipping settings for virtual products.

We haven't looked at orders yet, but it's worth mentioning that any orders that are composed entirely of downloadable and virtual products will be automatically marked as completed.

 Most users don't have to change the download default settings but, if you want to take a look, they are all available in the WordPress admin under **WooCommerce | Settings | Products | Downloadable Products**.

Adding global product attributes

In addition to using categories and tags similar to WordPress posts, there's one extra way that you can categorize your products, and that is by using product attributes. Product attributes are things such as color, size, style, and so on. A simple product could have multiple attributes. A small red and blue t-shirt could have the following attributes: red, blue, and small.

Setting up global product attributes will make creating variable products easier down the road.

How to do it...

Make sure you already have a simple product in your store and proceed with the following steps:

1.   From the WordPress admin, go to **Products | Attributes**.

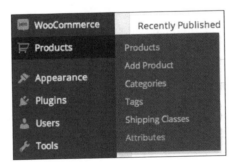

2. Under the **Add New Attribute** heading, you'll see settings to create attributes. The only mandatory field is **Name**.

3. Enter a name for the attribute and click on the **Add Attribute** button.

4. Now click on the icon on the far right in the Attribute table. When you hover over the button, you should see **Configure terms**.

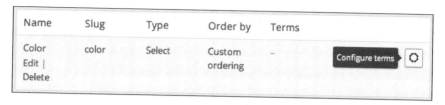

5. Enter a name for an attribute term. If your attribute is **Color**, then the attribute terms will be specific colors such as **red**, **black**, **blue**, **white**, and so on. Repeat this step for each attribute term. At the end, you should have a list of attribute terms.

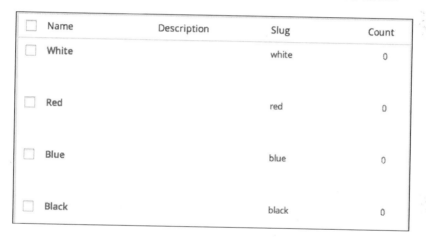

We've created a product attribute and some attribute terms. Now we can add them to our products.

1. From the WordPress admin, go to the **Product page** and click on **Edit** for any one of your products.

2. Under the **Product Data** panel, click on the **Attributes** tab.

3. You should see a drop-down with a list of attributes. Select your attribute and then click on the **Add** button.

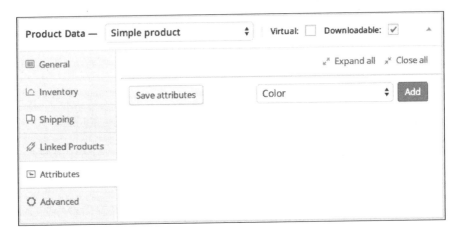

4. Start typing in the attributes that apply to this product. As you type, a suggestion tool will pop up that helps you select an attribute.

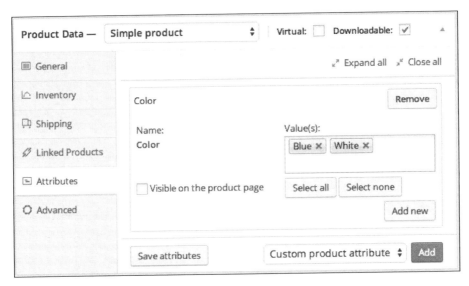

5. Now save your product by clicking on the **Update** button.

There's more...

If you check the **Visible on the product page** checkbox under the attribute you selected on the **Attributes** tab in the **Product Data** panel, these attributes will show up on the product page in an **Additional Information** tab.

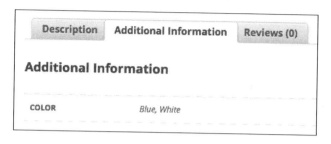

In *Chapter 3, Changing the Product Organization*, there's a recipe (*Adding filtered navigation with the Layered Nav widget*) that details how to filter your products with the Layered Nav widget. By adding attributes to your products, you make it easier for users to navigate your store and search for your products.

Adding a variable product

One of the complexities of e-commerce stores is figuring out how to sell similar products; for example, the same t-shirt design in different sizes and colors. Do you sell each size and color as a separate product with its own product page or do you combine them somehow?

WooCommerce handles this with **variable products**. Variable products can have multiple attributes such as size and color to help you sell these products. Throughout this chapter, I've been creating a poster product and attributes. I'm going to use the same data in this recipe as well, except that this time I'm going to create a variable product so people can choose the color of the poster.

Getting ready

You'll need to have set up global product attributes in the preceding recipe.

How to do it...

There are two basic parts to this. The first part is setting up the attributes this variation will use to distinguish between the different variations. The second part will define how each variation is different.

1. From the WordPress admin, go to **Products | Add Product**.

2. Just as with a simple product, add the **Product name** and **Featured Image**.

3. Scroll down to the **Product Data** panel and, from the drop-down, select **Variable product**. You may notice a few of the settings in the panel have been moved around.

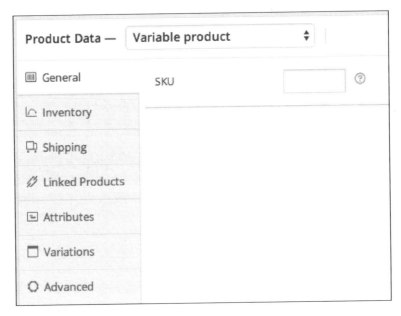

4. Click on the **Attributes** tab. You have to add attributes before you can add variations.

5. Select one of the global product attributes we created in the previous recipe and click on **Add.**

6. The poster I'm creating comes in blue and red. I'm going to select those attribute terms.

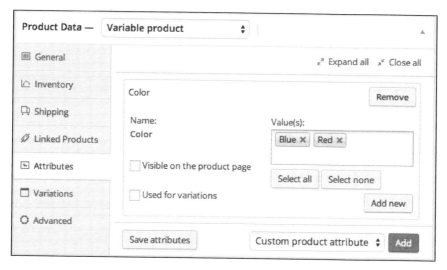

7. Click on the **Used for variations** checkbox.

8. Click on the **Save attributes** button.

By this point, we've told WooCommerce the attributes we're using to distinguish between the different variations. Now it's time to create our variations and tell WooCommerce how each one is different.

1. Click on the **Variations** tab in the **Product Data** panel.

2. Click on **Add Variation**.

3. Select your attribute in the drop-down, enter a price, and upload an image for that variation.

4. Repeat this for as many variations as you have. For my example, I'll be doing it one more time for the red variation.

5. Once you're all done, click on **Publish**.

 If you view the product on the frontend of your site, you'll notice how the featured image and price will change when selecting different attributes.

Adding an extra fee to a product with the Product Add-ons plugin

Variable products are incredibly powerful and you can do a lot with them. In some situations where you have a ton of extras or add-ons, it doesn't make sense to make a variation for each one. In such cases, it's easier to use a separate plugin that WooThemes has created, called **Product Add-ons**.

Getting ready

You'll need to have installed and activated the Product Add-ons plugin available at `http://www.woothemes.com/products/product-add-ons/`.

You should also have a product in your store.

How to do it...

We can add an add-on cost with the help of the following steps:

1. From the WordPress admin, go to the **Products** page and click on **Edit** for any one of your products.

2. Scroll down to the **Product Data** panel and click on the **Add-ons** tab.

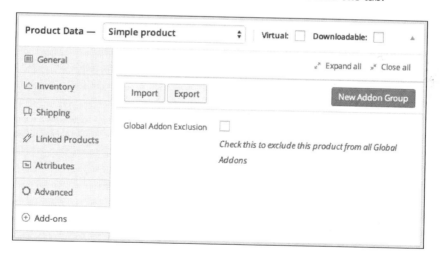

3. Click on the **New Addon Group** button.

4. Type in the name of the add-on group. If you're selling frames for your poster, you probably want to call it `Frame`.

5. You can now add as many options as you want. Make sure you enter a label and price for each one.

6. Click on the **Update** button.

You now have plenty of options to choose from on the frontend.

There's more...

There are different ways to use add-ons. With frames for a poster, it might make sense to only let the user choose one add-on. In such cases, you can change the **Group "Frame"** setting to use **Radio buttons** instead of **Checkboxes**.

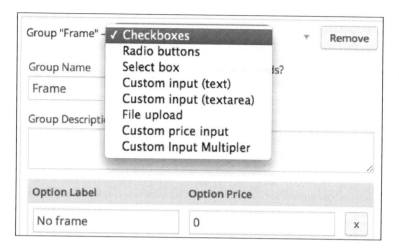

Adding a product bundle with the Product Bundles plugin

One of the most common ways through which both physical stores and e-commerce stores get more orders is by bundling products together and providing the customer with a discount. This can actually be a bit tricky in e-commerce if you don't set it up correctly. You'll most likely want to count the products independently for accounting, inventory, and reporting purposes. That's why there's a **Product Bundles** extension that handles all of that stuff while the customer just sees a product and the **Buy** button.

Getting ready

You'll need to have installed and activated the Product Bundles plugin available here: http://www.woothemes.com/products/product-bundles/. You should also have at least two simple products in your store.

How to do it...

In order to add a product bundle, carry out the following steps:

1. From the WordPress admin, go to **Products | Add Product**.

2. Give the product a name in the **Product Name** field.

3. Scroll down to the **Product Data** pane. From the drop-down, select **Product bundle**.

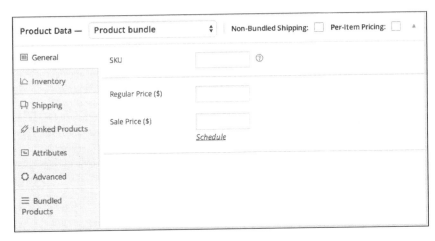

4. If your products are packaged separately, check the **Non-Bundled Shipping** checkbox.

5. Enter a price for the bundle in the **Regular Price ($)** field.

6. Click on the **Bundled Products** tab.

7. Under **Bundled Products**, type in the products that will make up the bundle.

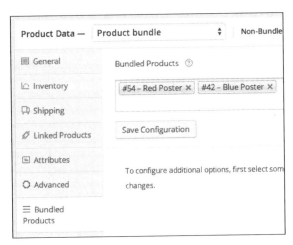

8. Click on **Save Configuration**.

9. After the configuration is saved, you can click on each component and adjust several details such as the quantity in each bundle. Adjusting these details is optional.

10. Publish your product and take a look at it from the frontend of your site.

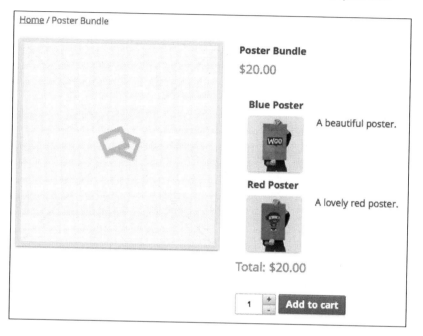

There's more...

You'll want to go back and add a featured image, and possibly an image gallery, for the bundle. It's really helpful to show the user exactly what they're getting in the bundle so make sure the featured image shows all of the items in the bundle.

Bundles are one of the more common ways of combining products, but there are other ways. For a full guide on the many ways of doing this, see the comparison article at `http://docs.woothemes.com/document/chained-products-vs-product-bundles-vs-force-sells-vs-grouped-products/`.

Bulk-uploading products with a CSV File

By now, you should have a pretty good idea of how you can configure your products. You're probably ready to set up all of your products and get this WooCommerce site up-and-running! If you only have a handful of products, I encourage you to do so. If you have hundreds or thousands of products, you can save yourself a whole lot of time by learning how to upload products in bulk.

Getting ready

You'll need to have installed and activated the **Product CSV Import Suite** plugin, available at `http://www.woothemes.com/products/product-csv-import-suite/`.

You should also have a simple product in your store.

There are free CSV uploaders in the WordPress.org repository that you could use. I would, however, advise caution. They're not as well maintained and, if there is a bug, your database could be filled with thousands of records that clutter everything up.

How to do it...

There's a trick to uploading your products that most people aren't aware of. It adds an extra step in the beginning, but it makes the whole process much easier. The first part is actually exporting some products from your store. By exporting them, you'll know the exact format you have to use to upload them.

1. From the WordPress admin, go to **WooCommerce | CSV Import Suite**.

2. Click on the **Export Products** tab.

   There are a bunch of settings on this page. You could very easily limit how many products are exported. This isn't really a concern for new stores. If you have a 100 or fewer products, just export everything.

3. Click on **Export Products**. A `woocommerce-product-export.csv` file should be saved to your computer.

4. Now open the downloaded file with your favorite calculation program. I like Sheets in Google Docs, but you could also use Microsoft Excel or Numbers for Macs.

	A	B	C	D	E	F
1	post_title	post_name	ID	post_excerpt	post_content	post_status
2	Apple	apple	33			publish
3	Blue Poster	poster	42	A beautiful poste	A much longer d	publish
4	WooThemes Pos	woothemes-post	50			publish
5	Red Poster	red-poster	54	A lovely red poster.		publish
6	Poster Bundle	poster-bundle	56			publish

You can now use the existing products in your exported file as a template for new products. I have a red poster and a blue poster in my sheet. I'm going to use those as a template for a green poster.

> You can leave the ID and `post_date` fields blank. They will be automatically calculated.

Now that you have your CSV file created, you can upload it. Follow these steps:

1. From the WordPress admin, go to **WooCommerce | CSV Import Suite**.
2. Click on the **Import Products** button.
3. Click on the **Choose File** button and select the file from your computer.

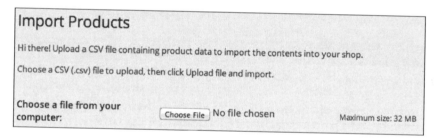

Import Products

Hi there! Upload a CSV file containing product data to import the contents into your shop.

Choose a CSV (.csv) file to upload, then click Upload file and import.

Choose a file from your computer: [Choose File] No file chosen   Maximum size: 32 MB

> At this point, you'll see a screen asking you to map fields from your CSV file to the fields in the database. If you exported a CSV file first, you shouldn't have to map any fields. It still is worth a quick check to make sure the fields in the CSV file are matching the fields in the database.

4. Click on **Submit** at the bottom of the page and wait for the products to upload.

There's more...

The CSV Import Suite can import either only simple products or only variable products. Don't try to import both at the same time. The steps are almost identical. Instead of clicking on the **Import Products** button on the CSV Import Suite screen, you must click on the **Import Variations** button.

 The process of uploading variable products is slightly different and is documented at http://docs.woothemes.com/ document/product-csv-import-suite-importing- product-variations/.

Removing product tabs

WooCommerce prints out all of the information about your products, which is generally pretty useful information for your customers. Sometimes, however, you may want to hide some of that information. With a bit of code, it's pretty easy to hide the product tabs.

Getting ready

You should have a simple product in your store.

How to do it...

To remove product tabs, we perform the following steps:

1. Go to one of your products and find the tabs near the bottom of the product page, underneath the products' short description and the buy button.

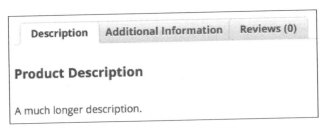

2. Use a tool that allows you to browse the source of an HTML page. I'm using Google Chrome's Inspect Element; you could also use **Firebug** from FireFox.

3. You should be able to find `tabs` in the source code.

```
<div class="woocommerce-tabs">
▼ <ul class="tabs">
    ::before
  ▶ <li class="description_tab active">...</li>
  ▶ <li class="additional_information_tab">...</li>
  ▶ <li class="reviews_tab">...</li>
    ::after
  </ul>
```

4. Write down any of the classes of the tabs you want to hide. Omit the `_tab` syntax at the end of the class. You just need the first part.

5. Now that we have the classes, we can write some code to hide those tabs. In your theme's `functions.php` file, add the following code:

```
add_filter( 'woocommerce_product_tabs',
'woocommerce_cookbook_remove_product_tabs', 10 );
function woocommerce_cookbook_remove_product_tabs( $tabs )
{
    return $tabs;
}
```

6. Now, in the `woocommerce_cookbook_remove_product_tabs` function, we have to specify exactly which tabs we want to remove. Just before the `return $tabs;` line, add the following code:

```
unset( $tabs['description'] );
```

7. Replace `description` with the class of the tab you want to remove. For example, it could read `unset( $tabs['description'] );` or `unset( $tabs[additional_information] );` or something else based on extra plugins adding more tabs.

8. Save the file and upload it to your site.

How it works...

The `woocommerce_product_tabs` filter allows you to add, rearrange, or remove tabs to suit your liking.

There's more...

It's actually a best practice to put this code in its own plugin rather than in your theme's `functions.php` file. For more details, refer to the *Creating a WooCommerce plugin* recipe in *Chapter 1, WooCommerce Basics*.

Reordering product tabs

You may not want to remove product tabs entirely. You may only want to rearrange them. That can also be done with a bit of code.

Getting ready

You should know how to find the product tab ID. This is discussed in the first part of the preceding recipe, *Removing product tabs*.

How to do it...

To reorder product tabs, take a look at the following steps:

1. Open up your theme's `functions.php` file, or a custom WooCommerce plugin that you have created, and paste in the following:

```
add_filter( 'woocommerce_product_tabs',
'woocommerce_cookbook_reorder_tabs', 98 );
function woocommerce_cookbook_reorder_tabs( $tabs )
{
    return $tabs;
}
```

2. In the `woocommerce_cookbook_reorder_tabs` function, you'll want to paste in the new order. Add the following code before the `return $tabs;` statement:

```
if( isset( $tabs['reviews']['priority'] ) ){
    $tabs['reviews']['priority'] = 10;
}
if( isset( $tabs['description']['priority'] ) ){
    $tabs['description']['priority'] = 20;
}
if( isset( $tabs['additional_information']['priority'] ) ){
    $tabs['additional_information']['priority'] = 30;
}
```

Downloading the example code

You can download the example code files for all Packt books you have purchased from your account at `http://www.packtpub.com`. If you purchased this book elsewhere, you can visit `http://www.packtpub.com/support` and register to have the files e-mailed directly to you.

3. To make one tab appear before another, make sure it has a lower priority. In this case, we're making the reviews tab show up first, then the description, and finally the additional information tab.

4. Save your file(s) and upload them. The product tabs should be rearranged.

How it works...

Just as in the preceding recipe, the `woocommerce_product_tabs` filter allows us to remove or alter the product tabs. In this case, we're only setting the priority of each tab. We aren't altering any other data.

3
Changing the Product Organization

In this chapter, we will cover:

- ▶ Changing the number of products per page
- ▶ Changing the number of columns on the Shop page
- ▶ Adding filtered navigation with the Layered Nav widget
- ▶ Making the Add to Cart button go straight to the checkout page
- ▶ Adding a custom tab to the product page
- ▶ Adding social media sharing icons to your product page
- ▶ Adding a Product Search widget
- ▶ Allowing users to search by SKU
- ▶ Adding extra sorting options on the Shop Page
- ▶ Sorting products from the oldest to the most recent
- ▶ Adding a site-wide notice
- ▶ Displaying the amount saved for on-sale products
- ▶ Displaying the amount saved as a percentage
- ▶ Changing the breadcrumb separator

Introduction

In *Chapter 2, Adding Products*, we were able to add all sorts of products to your store. Now that you have products in your store, it's time to customize your product page exactly the way you want. We'll be adding more tabs, changing sale prices, adding social media icons, adding special search bars, and much more. WooCommerce is incredibly modular and extendable. That's why there are so many free plugins on WordPress.org. We'll be configuring a lot of free plugins and, when there isn't a free plugin available, we'll look at achieving what we want with a line or two of code.

At the end of this chapter, you should have your product and category pages customized to your liking. In *Chapter 4, Running a Membership Site*, we'll talk more about membership sites and how they work.

Changing the number of products per page

WooCommerce assumes you have dozens of products in your store. For that reason, the layout is four products across and 10 products per page. That's a really nice format for most stores. But for some stores that have very few products or stores that have thousands and thousands, you may want to change that format.

Getting ready

You need to have a few products on your site, otherwise you won't be able to see any of the changes.

How to do it...

In order to change the number of products per page, go through the following steps:

1. In the WordPress admin, click on the **Plugins** menu and then on **Add New**.
2. Run a search for **WooCommerce Product Archive Customiser**.
3. Install and activate the plugin.
4. Once we have the plugin installed, it's time to configure it. Under **WooCommerce | Settings | Products | Display**, you'll find a new **Product Archives** settings section. Change the **Products per page** setting to 20.
5. Scroll down to the bottom of the page and click on the **Save changes** button.

There's more...

There are plenty more settings included in the **WooCommerce Product Archive Customizer** that you can play with. It's incredibly easy, for example, to change the number of columns, add a badge to new products, or hide reviews.

Changing the number of columns on the Shop page

You can do a lot with the free plugins available at WordPress.org, without any developer skills or with a limited budget, and this is probably the right course of action. If, however, you have time to dig into the code, then you can sometimes get modest speed increases by writing a few lines of code instead of loading a big plugin. With this recipe, I'm going to show you how to change the number of columns on your shop page without a plugin. We're going to code it manually.

Getting ready

You'll need to have a few products on your site so that you can see how the columns rearrange.

How to do it...

In order to change the number of columns on the **Shop** page, go through the following steps:

1. Open up your theme's `functions.php` file, located under `wp-content/themes/your-theme-name/`. Optionally, you could create your own custom WooCommerce plugin as instructed in the *Creating a WooCommerce plugin* recipe in *Chapter 1, WooCommerce Basics*.

2. In it, we're only going to add four lines of code:

```
add_filter( 'loop_shop_columns',
'woocommerce_cookbook_loop_shop_columns', 20 );
function woocommerce_cookbook_loop_shop_columns( $cols ) {
    return 3;
}
```

If you save and upload this file, you'll notice that there are three columns, but they don't look very good because we haven't changed our CSS. To make this look nice, we have to alter our CSS to match.

3. Open up your theme's `style.css` stylesheet so we can add some extra styles.

4. Paste in the following code at the bottom of your stylesheet:

```
.woocommerce ul.products li.product, .woocommerce-page
ul.products li.product{
    width: 30.75%
}
```

5. Save the file and upload it.

Your columns should now fill the available space.

Most themes add extra margins and padding on your products. For that reason, you need to leave an extra buffer in your calculations. That's why, for three products, I chose to use 30.75 percent instead of 33.3 percent. You can tweak the width value until you get it just right.

There's more...

Some custom themes use **pluggable functions**. If the number of columns isn't changing, there are some alternative ways to write this code so that it works with pluggable functions. You can find a few examples at `http://docs.woothemes.com/document/change-number-of-products-per-row/`.

Adding filtered navigation with the Layered Nav widget

When you have thousands, hundreds, or even dozens of products, it becomes very important to give your customers enhanced search functionality to find the product they want. One of the ways of doing that is to give them a way to filter search results. WooCommerce has filtering logic built right into it with the **Layered Nav widget**.

Getting ready

You'll need to have a few products on your site and at least some of those products will need to have **global attributes** set as per the *Adding global product attributes* recipe in *Chapter 2, Adding Products*.

How to do it...

If your products already have attributes set, then giving your customer the ability to filter the shop page or search page is very easy. You only need to add the Layered Navigation widget to the page.

1. Go to **Appearance | Widgets**.
2. Under **Available Widgets**, click on **WooCommerce Layered Nav** and then add it to the appropriate sidebar.

> WordPress themes can have multiple sidebars, and they vary on a per-theme basis. If you don't know which sidebar to use, a good place to start is by trying the main sidebar or primary sidebar. If you are still having problems, then the next best bet is to try each sidebar until you find the right one.

3. Once the widget is added to a sidebar, it should slide open. At this point, you can change the **Title**, **Attribute**, and **Display** type. The defaults are perfectly good for this example, so I won't be changing them.

4. Click on the **Save** button.

5. Go to the frontend of your store and you should see the Layered Nav widget.

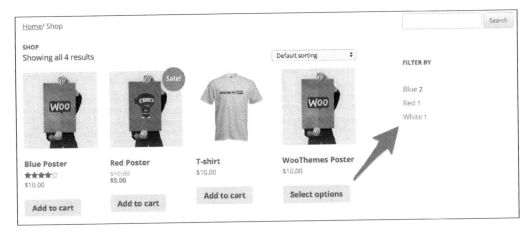

> I highly advise putting the Layered Nav widget near the top of the widgets so that your users can see it without having to scroll down.

There's more...

In addition to the Layered Nav widget, which is great for attributes such as color and size, there's also a **WooCommerce Price Filter** that is great for letting a customer only see products in their price range. There is also the **WooCommerce Layered Nav Filters**, useful when you have a ton of Layered Nav widgets. With this, users can see all of the filters in one place and disable them easily.

These widgets only work on pages that display a list of products, such as the **Shop** page. The widgets won't do anything or even show up on a page that doesn't display products.

Making the Add to Cart button go straight to the checkout page

On the flip side of having hundreds or thousands of products, you may only have one product, at which point the cart becomes pretty useless. In that case, you can actually have a customer skip right over the cart and land on your checkout page. It's one less step the customer has to make and keeps them focused on checking out rather than cruising the site, which should increase conversions.

 We have covered a similar recipe, *Skipping the cart and going straight to checkout*, in *Chapter 7, Modifying the Checkout Process*, which uses code instead of a plugin.

Getting ready

You'll need to have a product in your store.

How to do it...

This is a feature a lot of store owners have asked for, so there are several prebuilt solutions out there. We'll be using a plugin from WordPress.org that is quite straightforward and simple with no options, named **Skip Cart WooCommerce**.

1. In the WordPress admin, click on the **Plugins** menu and then on **Add New**.
2. Run a search for **Skip Cart WooCommerce**.
3. Install and activate the plugin.
4. Now go to the frontend of your site and add a product to your cart. This action will automatically take you to the checkout page.

 At the time of writing, there is a PHP warning in this plugin. It will most likely be fixed by the time of publication. They aren't serious issues, so you can simply hide the warnings by disabling WP_DEBUG in your config file. For more information, refer to http://codex.wordpress.org/WP_DEBUG.

There's more...

You may notice that the button says **Add to Cart**, but there technically isn't a cart. If you wanted, you could change the product button to **Checkout** or something similar. This can be achieved with some code snippets available at WooThemes.com. For more information, refer to http://docs.woothemes.com/document/change-add-to-cart-button-text/.

Adding a custom tab to the product page

For most businesses, you can put all of the product information you need into the description field. For some industries, you may have extra information you want to add to the product page. One of the best ways to add this information is by adding an extra tab to the product page. That way, it's not in the way but it's still accessible.

Getting ready

You need to have a product in your store.

How to do it...

The first part of setting this up is installing the right plugin.

1. In the WordPress admin, click on the **Plugins** menu and then on **Add New**.

2. Run a search for **WooCommerce Custom Product Tabs Lite**.

3. Install and activate the plugin.

4. Now that we have the plugin activated, it's time to configure it. Go to the **Products** menu in the WordPress admin and select one of your products.

5. Under the **Product Data** tab, click on **Custom Tab**. From here, you can add a title and whatever content you like. It could be an embed code from a site such as YouTube, HTML, or plain text. It's entirely up to you.

6. Click on the **Update** button.

7. Go to the frontend of your site and look at the tab with the content you entered.

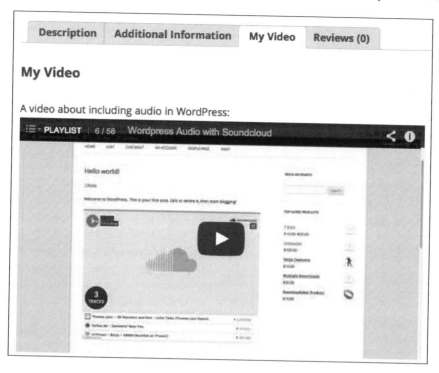

There's more...

This plugin is really simple, which is great for people who are just getting started. If you want a few more customization options, there is a premium version of this plugin available on WooThemes.com. It gives you more control over the tab order on a per product level or on a site-wide level.

Adding social media sharing icons to your product page

There are a ton of social media sharing plugins for WordPress. Unfortunately, not all of them work very well with WooCommerce. With this recipe, we'll be installing a plugin and telling the plugin exactly where we want our social media icons so that they look nice on our product page.

Getting ready

You need to have a product in your store.

How to do it...

The first part is installing the plugin. We'll be installing **Jetpack**, which is built and managed by WordPress.com. After we get it installed, we only need very minor tweaks to make it work well with WooCommerce.

1. In the WordPress admin, click on the **Plugins** menu and then on **Add New**.

2. Run a search for **Jetpack by WordPress.com**.

3. Install and activate the plugin.

4. In the WordPress admin, click on the newly created **Jetpack** menu and then on the **Settings** submenu.

 Jetpack is known to have a lot of functionality built in. You'll want to look through what's possible and enable it. We only need to turn on the **Sharing** module.

5. Enable the **Sharing** module.

☐ ‹/› Markdown	
☐ ▢ Mobile Theme	
☐ 🔍 Omnisearch	
☐ ↻ Sharing	Activate
☐ ≡ Shortcode Embeds	
☐ 🌐 Site Icon	
☐ 🗎 Site Verification	

6. Now that it's enabled, you'll have to configure it. Scroll down to the same **Sharing** module, hover over it, and click on **Configure**.

   At this point, you'll see a settings page with various options. The first step is to select which services you want listed on your site. You can pick as many as you like.

7. Drag-and-drop services from **Available Services** to **Enabled Services**.

8. Make sure the social media icons will be shown on the product pages.

9. Click on **Save Changes**.

   If you went to a product page on your site right now, you'd see the social media icons, but they're all the way at the bottom of the product page – even beneath the description and additional information tabs. With a bit of custom coding, we can put them exactly where we want them.

10. Add the following code to your theme's `functions.php` file, located under `wp-content/themes/your-theme-name/`, or your custom WooCommerce plugin:

```
add_action( 'woocommerce_share',
'woocommerce_cookbook_social_share_icons', 10 );
function woocommerce_cookbook_social_share_icons() {
    if ( function_exists( 'sharing_display' ) ) {
```

```
            remove_filter( 'the_content', 'sharing_display', 19
    );
            remove_filter( 'the_excerpt', 'sharing_display', 19
    );
            echo sharing_display();
        }
    }
```

All done! Load up your product page and see the social media icons right beneath the **Add to cart** button.

How it works...

The Jetpack plugin handles social media sharing and icons. The code we wrote moves the output from Jetpack to exactly where we want it to be.

The first part of the code adds extra functionality on the WooCommerce product page. Within that code, we remove the old Jetpack output and print out new output. The elegant part of this code is that the Jetpack output only changes on the WooCommerce product pages. You could use the same social sharing functionality for your blog posts and the social sharing buttons will appear at the end of the post, which, of course, is controlled through Jetpack.

Adding a Product Search widget

There are a number of tools built into WooCommerce that people don't even know about. One of those tools is the **Product Search widget**. It works in a very similar way to the default search widget in WordPress, except that this one only searches for products. It won't show any results for your pages, posts, or other custom post types.

Additionally, the results it does show are displayed as they would appear on the shop page. This will usually look better than the standard search page. If you have a site that's primarily an e-commerce site, I recommend using the Product Search widget so your users can find what they want a little faster.

How to do it...

To add a product search widget, let's have a look at the following steps:

1. Go to **Appearance** | **Widgets**.
2. Under **Available Widgets**, click on **WooCommerce Product Search** and then add it to the appropriate sidebar.
3. You may optionally add a **Title** to the widget.
4. Click on **Save**.

There's more...

The default Product Search widget that comes with WooCommerce is already very useful. If you want to have instant search results as you type or if you want to control the search algorithm, there is the WooCommerce Product Search extension available at `http://www.woothemes.com/products/woocommerce-product-search/`.

Allowing users to search by SKU

One of the best things about WooCommerce is how simple it is. The developers purposefully don't include every possibility because it makes the interface too confusing. One of the settings that some people do end up needing that's not included in WooCommerce is the ability to run a search for a product by **SKU**. Luckily, there's a free plugin on WordPress.org that can enhance the WooCommerce Product Search widget with this functionality.

Getting ready

Make sure you have the WooCommerce Product Search widget set on one of your pages.

How to do it...

In order to allow users to search by SKU, go through the following steps:

1. In the WordPress admin, click on the **Plugins** menu and then on **Add New**.
2. Run a search for **Search by SKU for WooCommerce**.
3. Install and activate the plugin.

How it works...

The **Search by SKU for WooCommerce** plugin is one of those plugins that does just one thing and does it very well. There are no settings to configure—it just works.

There's more...

There are more of these plugins available for free on WordPress.org. Another popular variation of this plugin is the **Search by Product Tag for WooCommerce** plugin made by the same author.

Adding extra sorting options on the Shop page

When you're on the WooCommerce shop page or on any of the category pages, there are five ways to sort your products: **popularity, average rating, newness, price low to high,** and **price high to low**. That's a pretty good range of ways to sort your products. Of course, it doesn't cover every possibility. You may want to have your products randomly sorted, sorted by products on sale, or sorted alphabetically.

As is typically the case with WordPress, someone has already thought of all of these and bundled them into a free plugin.

How to do it...

This is a pretty quick process. First, we'll have to install the plugin.

1. In the WordPress admin, click on the **Plugins** menu and then on **Add New**.
2. Run a search for **WooCommerce Extra Product Sorting Options**.

3. Install and activate the plugin.

   Now that we've installed the plugin, we have to configure a few settings.

4. From the WordPress admin, go to **WooCommerce | Settings | Products | Display**.

5. The plugin gives you the ability to rename the default sorting option with the **New Default Sorting Label** field. You could name it as something more intuitive to the user; for example, `Our Selection`.

6. Just beneath the **New Default Sorting Label** field, you'll see the **Add Product Sorting Options** label and several checkboxes. Check as many as you like.

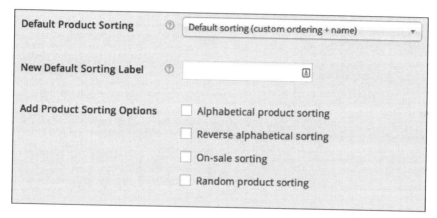

You might be tempted to give the user all of the options. This isn't necessarily a good idea. The more options you give to users, the more time they'll have to spend processing each option trying to choose one. It's best to include only the options that are most frequently requested.

How it works...

This plugin uses a bunch of WooCommerce hooks to modify the default ordering. In the next recipe, we'll write some code that interacts with these hooks.

Sorting products from the oldest to the most recent

If the preceding recipe doesn't give you enough options to sort your products, you can add custom code to meet your needs. With a bit of code, you can sort products from the oldest to the most recent.

How to do it...

We'll need to add two pieces of custom code. The first piece of code will add an option to the sorting drop-down.

1. Add the following code at the bottom of your theme's `functions.php` file under `wp-content/themes/your-theme-name/` or in your custom WooCommerce plugin:

```
// Add a new sorting option
add_filter( 'woocommerce_default_catalog_orderby_options',
'woocommerce_cookbook_catalog_orderby' );
add_filter( 'woocommerce_catalog_orderby',
'woocommerce_cookbook_catalog_orderby' );
function woocommerce_cookbook_catalog_orderby( $sortby ) {
    $sortby['oldest_to_newest'] = __( 'Sort by oldest to
newest', 'woocommerce' );
    return $sortby;
}
```

This code should add a new option to the sorting drop-down.

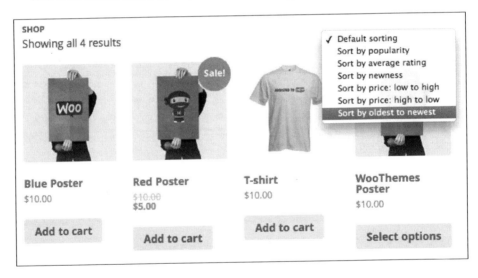

Unfortunately, WooCommerce doesn't know what to do with that value. We still need to add a bit more code to tell WooCommerce exactly how to process that information.

2. Add the following code beneath the code you pasted in the preceding step:

```
// Add sorting oldest to newest functionality to sorting dropdown
add_filter( 'woocommerce_get_catalog_ordering_args',
'woocommerce_cookbook_get_catalog_ordering_args' );
function woocommerce_cookbook_get_catalog_ordering_args(
$args ) {
    // get the orderby value
    $orderby_value = isset( $_GET['orderby'] ) ? wc_clean(
$_GET['orderby'] ) : apply_filters(
'woocommerce_default_catalog_orderby', get_option(
'woocommerce_default_catalog_orderby' ) );
    // if the orderby value matches our custom option
    if ( 'oldest_to_newest' == $orderby_value ) {
        $args['orderby'] = 'date'; $args['order'] = 'ASC';
    }
    return $args;
}
```

3. Save the file and upload it to your site.

Now, if you click on the new option, which we created in the preceding code from the sorting drop-down, the page will reload and the items will be rearranged according to the new order.

How it works...

The actual functionality happens in the `woocommerce_cookbook_get_catalog_ordering_args` function. In there, we determine the `$orderby_value`, which is basically checking which option is set in the drop-down. After we have the value selected, we check whether that's our custom option. If it is our custom option, then we change the sort order.

There's more...

In the code we pasted in, you'll notice the `$args` array with two keys: `orderby` and `order`. A developer can change the values in that array to implement any custom sort order.

Adding a site-wide notice

There may be times when you have something you need every customer to see. Maybe you're having a limited-time sale, a problem with your contact page, or you just announced an awesome new product. For these types of situations, WooCommerce includes a setting to enable a site-wide notice.

How to do it...

To add a site-wide notice, perform the following steps:

1. From the WordPress admin, go to **WooCommerce | Settings**.

2. Check the **Store Notice** checkbox that can be found under the **General Options** heading.

3. Once you check the box, you'll see a **Store Notice Text** field appear. Fill this in with any content you want.

4. Click on the **Save changes** button at the bottom of the page.

5. Visit your site and see the notice.

There's more...

If you need a bit more control over the notice, there are several free notice plugins on the WordPress.org repository. The Simple Notices plugin has a bit more flexibility with color choices and has title and description fields.

There is also the **WooCommerce Cart Notices** plugin, which adds notices depending on what's in the user's cart. We take a look at this plugin in the *Adding banners to remind customers of upgrades* recipe in *Chapter 7, Modifying the Checkout Process*.

Displaying the amount saved for on-sale products

WooCommerce will automatically add a sale badge to any products on-sale. That way, a customer browsing your store will be able to see at a glance which products are on-sale. If you have a store that has sales pretty often or where some products have a big discount and others have a small discount, you might want to give the customer more information. Replacing the sale badge with a badge that shows the discount amount can be really useful in these situations.

Getting ready

Make sure you have a product in your store that's on-sale. This can be set in the **Sale Price** field in the **Product Data** panel on the **Edit Product** screen in the WordPress admin.

How to do it...

There's a plugin that will do all of this for us. There aren't any settings to be configured. Just install and activate the plugin and it's done.

1. In the WordPress admin, click on the **Plugins** menu and then on **Add New**.
2. Run a search for **WooCommerce Smart Sale Badge**.
3. Install and activate the plugin.
4. Take a look at the frontend of your site and view a product that's on sale.

If your sale badge doesn't look like mine or you don't see it at all, that's most likely something controlled in your theme. You can reach out to the theme developer for assistance or, if you're familiar with HTML and CSS, you can try styling it yourself.

There's more...

If you want to display percentages instead of an absolute dollar amount, we'll cover that in the next recipe.

Displaying the amount saved as a percentage

With higher ticket items, it's sometimes nice to show the customer the percentage saved versus the dollar amount. With two pieces of code, we can change this functionality.

Getting ready

Make sure you have a product in your store that's on sale.

How to do it...

Currently, the only way to do display the amount saved in a percentage is with a bit of custom code. You have to add the percentage saved to the HTML. This can be done with two small snippets.

1. In your code editor, open up your theme's `functions.php` file, located under `wp-content/themes/your-theme-name/`, or your custom WooCommerce plugin.

2. Add the following code to the bottom of that file:

```
// calculate the percentage saved.
function woocommerce_cookbook_calculate_percentage_saved(
$product ) {
    return round( ( ( $product->get_regular_price() -
$product->get_sale_price() ) / $product-
>get_regular_price() ) * 100 );
}
```

This piece of code calculates the percentage saved. Now we need to write a bit more code that will hook into the right part of the WooCommerce page and replace the default sale price with our new sale price, including the percentage saved.

3. Add the following code to the bottom of your file:

```
// Add percentage saved next to sale price
add_filter( 'woocommerce_sale_price_html',
'woocommerce_cookbook_percentage_saved', 10, 2 );
function woocommerce_cookbook_percentage_saved( $price,
$product ) {
    $percentage_saved =
woocommerce_cookbook_calculate_percentage_saved( $product
);
    return $price . sprintf( __( ' Save %s', 'woocommerce'
), $percentage_saved . '%' );
}
```

4. Save the file and upload it to your site.

5. You should now see the percentage saved where the sale price used to be.

There's more...

This recipe and the previous one both changed how the sale price was displayed. As you can see, they can be done in very different ways. A developer could combine these methods and get the best from both worlds. If you're looking to get started with customizing your WooCommerce site but don't know where to start, a good place would be the WooCommerce templates located in the /templates/ folder in the WooCommerce plugin. You can see all of the hooks used to display various pieces of functionality.

Changing the breadcrumb separator

One of the really useful features built into WooCommerce allows the customer to see where they are in the store and then click on a link and go back to a previously visited page. In the programming world, these are called **breadcrumbs**.

There are several hooks you can use to customize the breadcrumbs to your liking. We'll be using a little code snippet to change what the actual code looks like.

Getting ready

Make sure you have a product in your store and that it's in a product category. That way, you can see the breadcrumbs.

How to do it...

We'll need a little snippet of code to change the breadcrumb separator. We will also need to look up the HTML entity for the character we want to use. If you don't know what an HTML entity is, that's fine. Just know that certain characters (such as <, >, &, ©, and others) can't always be used directly in code. Sometimes, you need to help the computer translate those symbols. First, let's add the function we need.

1. Add the following code to your theme's `functions.php` file, located under `wp-content/themes/your-theme-name/`, or your custom WooCommerce plugin:

```
// Change the breadcrumb delimeter from '/' to '>'
add_filter( 'woocommerce_breadcrumb_defaults',
'woocommerce_cookbook_breadcrumb_delimiter' );
function woocommerce_cookbook_breadcrumb_delimiter(
$defaults ) {
}
```

At this point, we have a function, but it's not doing anything. We need to add a bit of logic to the function. Before we do that, we need to know the HTML entity of the character we want to use. We'll be using the > character. A quick Google search will reveal that the HTML entity for the > character is `&gt;`. Optionally, you can use a website such as `http://www.w3schools.com/html/html_entities.asp` to find the HTML entity you need. Now that we have the value we need, we put it in our function.

2. In the `woocommerce_cookbook_breadcrumb_delimiter` function, we just add the following code right after the beginning of the function:

```
$defaults['delimiter'] = ' &gt; ';
return $defaults;
```

3. Save your file and upload it to your site. You should see a new separator in your breadcrumbs.

There's more...

There are plenty of other breadcrumb settings we haven't covered. A useful free plugin that allows you to customize all of this without code is called **WooCommerce Breadcrumbs**. If you need more control, I'd advise you to use that plugin.

4

Running a Membership Site

In this chapter, we will cover:

- ▸ Adding a subscription product with the WooCommerce Subscriptions plugin
- ▸ Creating pricing tables with the Easy Pricing Tables plugin
- ▸ Adding member-only pricing with the Dynamic Pricing plugin
- ▸ Displaying special pricing for logged-in users with the Conditional Content plugin
- ▸ Creating members-only content
- ▸ Creating a members-only store
- ▸ Making subscription payments more consistent
- ▸ Customizing the subscription price string
- ▸ Creating a custom subscription interval
- ▸ Exporting subscription orders

Introduction

Now that we know how to add products to our store and customize the way it looks and is organized, it's time to branch out and look at how we can sell things other than t-shirts. Being able to bill someone every week, month, or year is incredibly challenging on a technical level. Many e-commerce platforms can't do it at all and the ones that do usually have high monthly fees and limitations. The **WooCommerce Subscriptions** plugin is phenomenally good at selling memberships and runs entirely on your own website, so you don't have to pay monthly fees.

Once you start billing people regularly, you can set up all types of membership sites: sites that have special pricing for members, sites that only allow members to purchase items, sites where members get access to premium content, and, of course subscription websites that will send users a package every week, month, or year.

The vast majority of the recipes in this chapter require the WooCommerce Subscriptions plugin (`http://www.woothemes.com/products/woocommerce-subscriptions/`), which is a premium extension for WooCommerce, to be installed and activated. Recurring billing is very complex and not all payment gateways work with Subscriptions. It's worth reading through the documentation located at `http://docs.woothemes.com/document/subscriptions/payment-gateways/#section-1` to make sure your payment gateway is compatible. Both Simplify Commerce and PayPal Standard, which are included in the WooCommerce core, are compatible with Subscriptions.

Adding a subscription product with the WooCommerce Subscriptions plugin

Before being able to bill someone regularly, we'll have to set up a product that has special subscription billing details. Subscription products are very similar to simple products and only take a few extra steps to set up.

Getting ready

You must have the WooCommerce Subscriptions plugin installed and activated on your website.

How to do it...

In order to add a subscription product with the help of WooCommerce Subscriptions, implement the following steps:

1. From the WordPress admin, go to **Products | Add New**.
2. Add a **Product name** and **Description** as you would for any other product.

3. Scroll down to the **Product Data** panel and change the product type to **Simple subscription**. You'll see several new fields appear.

4. For a subscription product, you must fill out the **Subscription Price ($)** field. The **Sign-up Fee** and **Free Trial** fields are optional. You can also change the billing period right next to the **Subscription Price** field.

5. Click on the **Publish** button.

You can now see your subscription product on the frontend of your site.

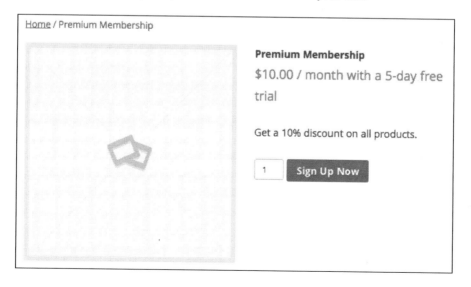

There's more...

You'll notice that in addition to the **Simple subscription** product type, there is a **Variable subscription** product type. These work just like **Variable Products**, with the added subscription fields. If you have very similar subscriptions, it may be worth putting them all under one **Variable subscription** product type to save space in your store.

Creating pricing tables with the Easy Pricing Tables plugin

If you're offering different subscriptions with similar features, it's really nice to help the customer understand which subscription is the right one for their budget. One of the best ways to do this is to create a pricing table that highlights the differences at a glance. The WordPress ecosystem already has a pricing tables plugin available for free on the WordPress. org plugin repository.

Getting ready

You must have the WooCommerce Subscriptions plugin installed and activated on your site. You should also have two Simple subscription products set up on your site.

How to do it...

There are three parts to this recipe. The first part of this recipe involves installing the right plugin.

1. From the WordPress admin, go to **Plugins | Add New**.
2. Run a search for the **Easy Pricing Tables Lite by Fatcat Apps** plugin.
3. Install and activate the plugin.

Now that we have the plugin installed, we need to create a pricing table.

1. In the WordPress admin, you'll see a new menu item called **Pricing Tables**. Go to **Pricing Tables | Add New**.

2. Enter a name for the pricing table.

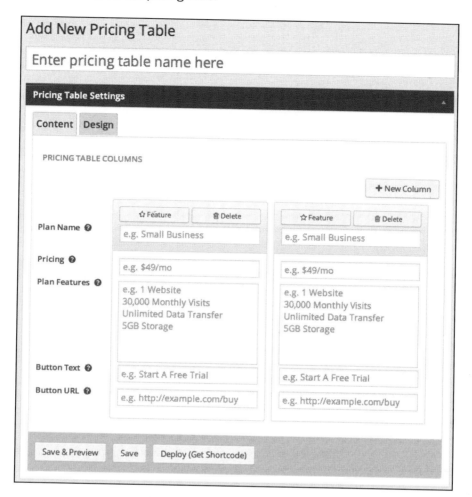

3. For each of your subscription products, you'll want to enter a **Plan Name**, **Pricing**, and **Plan Features** (one per line).

4. You should also fill in the **Button Text**, which can be something as simple as Subscribe.

5. Finally, you should fill in the **Button URL**. The easiest way to get the pricing table to work with WooCommerce is to enter the URL for your subscription product.

If you enter the the URL for your product page into the **Button URL**, that will take the customer to the subscription product page and they have to click one more time to add it to the cart. If you want it to be done in one step, you'll have to create a URL that automatically adds a product to the cart. It sounds complicated, but can be done in a step-by-step manner. I've already documented how to do this on my blog at: `http://speakinginbytes.com/2014/06/create-pricing-table-woocommerce/`.

6. Once you're done putting your product information into the pricing table, click on the **Save** button.

Now we have a pricing table, but we have to put it somewhere on our site.

1. Click on the **Deploy (Get Shortcode)** button. A pop-up will appear. Copy the shortcode from the pop-up.

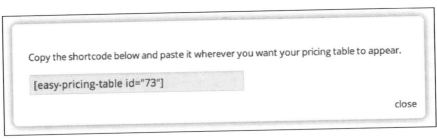

Copy the shortcode below and paste it wherever you want your pricing table to appear.

[easy-pricing-table id="73"]

close

2. You can now paste this shortcode into the content of any existing WordPress page or post and it will display the pricing table. You could, of course, create a new WordPress page or post if you like. Save the page and it should look something like the following screenshot:

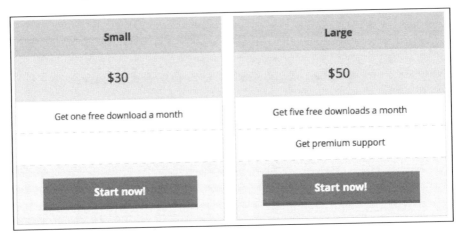

There's more...

You may notice when you install the Easy Pricing Tables plugin that there's a prompt for you to join a **Pricing Table Crash Course**. I highly recommend this crash course. It goes into the fundamentals of pricing and can help you convert more visitors into customers and also possibly raise your prices.

The Easy Pricing Tables plugin has some prebuilt styles that you can modify so you don't have to custom-code CSS. When you're editing the pricing table, you will see a **Design** tab. Click on that tab and take a look at all of the design options built into the plugin.

Adding member-only pricing with the Dynamic Pricing plugin

It's nice to give your regular customers a loyalty program that keeps them coming back and gives them some amount of brand loyalty. One of the ways of doing this with WooCommerce is to let customers buy a premium membership that gives them a percentage reduction on all sales. This can be achieved by combining the WooCommerce Subscriptions and Dynamic Pricing (http://www.woothemes.com/products/dynamic-pricing/) plugins. Of course, both are available at WooThemes.com.

Getting ready

You must have the WooCommerce Subscriptions plugin as well as the Dynamic Pricing plugin installed and activated on your site.

How to do it...

We'll be going into the Dynamic Pricing settings and configuring some price discounts for any user that is currently subscribed to a subscription.

1. In the WordPress admin, click on **WooCommerce** and then on **Dynamic Pricing**.

2. Click on **Roles**.

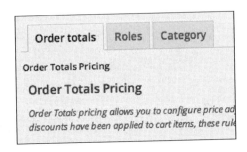

3. On the **Role Pricing** page, you can now set up special pricing rules for specific roles. The role we want to target is the **Subscriber** role. Enable special pricing for **Subscriber** and enter the type of discount and the amount.

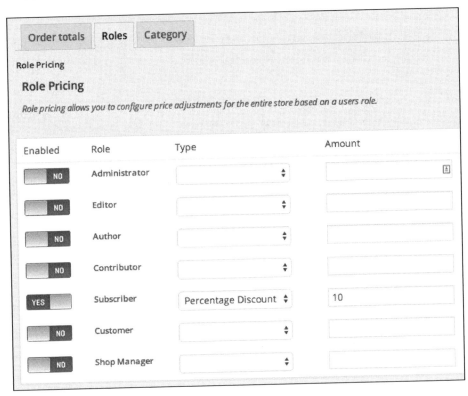

A subscriber will see a discount on the frontend.

 If you want to test whether the price discounts are working properly, it can be very helpful to add the pricing discount to the **Administrator** role. That way, you can see the price discount without having to buy your own subscription.

How it works...

WordPress already has the role functionality built into it, and the two plugins—WooCommerce Subscriptions and WooCommerce Dynamic Pricing—work together beautifully to take advantage of those roles. Subscriptions will automatically change a customer's role from **Customer** to **Subscriber** while their subscription is active and then change them back to a **Customer** after the subscription has expired or been cancelled. When a user is logged in, the Dynamic Pricing plugin will automatically calculate, and provide the user with, the correct price for their role.

There's more...

If you want to take this to the next level, Dynamic Pricing also integrates with the **Groups** plugin. You could look into using the free-of-charge Groups plugin (`https://wordpress.org/plugins/groups/`) with the premium Groups for WooCommerce plugin (`http://www.woothemes.com/products/groups-woocommerce/`) to create many different types of membership levels and discounts.

Displaying special pricing for logged-in users with the Conditional Content plugin

If you are using Dynamic Pricing or some other pricing plugin to create special prices for users, you should display that content to customers. This is especially useful if you have bulk pricing, where the discounts aren't automatically visible to customers. In this recipe, we're going to show a special message to customers who aren't a part of our premium membership and show them how much they could be saving if they were a premium member.

Getting ready

You must have WooCommerce Subscriptions, Dynamic Pricing, and Conditional Content (`http://www.woothemes.com/products/woocommerce-conditional-content/`) installed and activated on your site.

How to do it...

To display special pricing for logged-in users with conditional content, let's take a look at the following steps:

1. From the WordPress admin, go to **WooCommerce | Content Blocks**.
2. Click on **Add Content Block**.

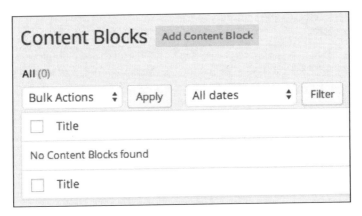

3. Enter a title for the content block and then add a description.

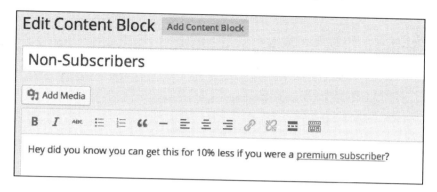

4. Now scroll down to the **Rules** panel. This is where we'll be using some conditional content logic to only display this message to non-subscribers. In our case, we'll want to create a rule that displays only when a user doesn't have the **Subscriber** role.

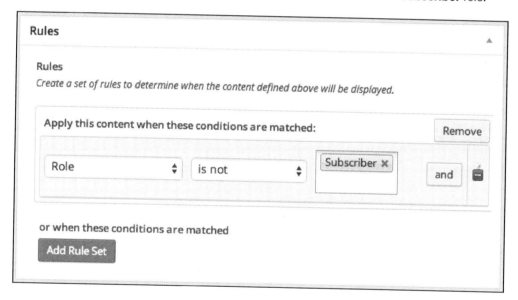

 You can combine as many rules as you like by clicking on the **and** button. You could, for example, add an extra rule to make sure this message doesn't appear for premium subscription products.

5. Click on **Publish**.

There's more...

You can not only control when this message is shown with this extension, but you can also control where it's shown. On the **Add Content Block** page, there's a panel in the sidebar called **Output Settings**. This allows you to choose how often and where the message gets displayed.

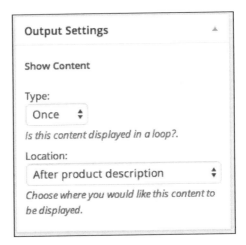

Creating members-only content

One of the many uses of WooCommerce is to create a membership site. Using a few extra plugins, you can create premium content that's only available to users who have purchased the correct products from your site. The nice thing about this setup is that, if you want your membership site to sell any products, it's really easy to add that functionality, whereas a typical membership plugin will only allow memberships.

Getting ready

You must have WooCommerce Subscriptions, Groups (free-of-charge on WordPress.org), and Groups for WooCommerce (premium, available at WooThemes.com) installed and activated on your site. You should also have a Simple subscription product already created.

How to do it...

We're going to use a free plugin called Groups, which allows us to group our users and restrict content to specific groups. After creating the groups and the content, we'll be connecting a product to a group with Groups for WooCommerce.

1. In the WordPress admin, click on **Groups**.

2. Go to **Groups | Capabilities**.

3. Click on **New Capability**.

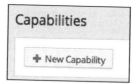

4. Add a name for this capability. Something like `Read premium posts` is a pretty good name.

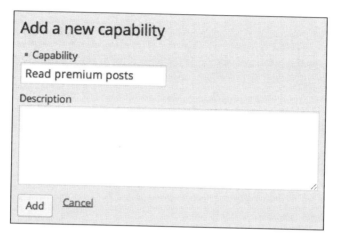

5. Click on the **Add** button.

6. Click on **New Group**.

7. Enter a **Name** for the group.

8. Enter the name for your group such as `Premium Content` will work well.

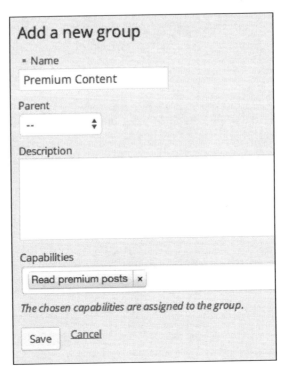

9. Click on the **Save** button.

We've created a group and a capability. We need to tell Groups that this capability can be used to restrict access.

1. Go to **Groups | Options**.
2. Under **Capabilities**, add the new capability we have created.

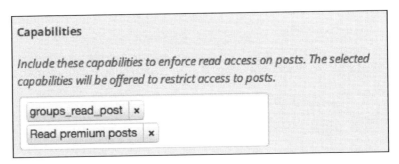

At this point, we've created a group, created a capability, assigned that capability to a group, and told Groups the capability can be used to restrict content. Let's create a page that only that group can access:

1. Go to **Pages | Add New**.

2. Add a title and content as you would on any other WordPress page.

3. In the sidebar, you should see an **Access restrictions** panel. Here, you can enter the capability you have created.

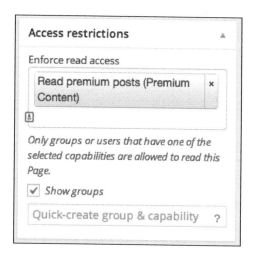

4. Click on **Publish**.

Alright. At this point, we've successfully restricted the page to our premium group.

 If you log out of your site and try again, there should be no way for you to access the page. It shouldn't appear in the menus and, if you access the URL directly, you should hit a 404 page.

Now we need to connect a product to the group we have created.

1. In the WordPress admin, click on **Products** and navigate to an existing subscription product in your store.

2. Scroll down to the **Product Data** panel.

3. Click on the **Groups** tab.

4. In the **Add to Groups** field, enter the name of the group you created earlier.

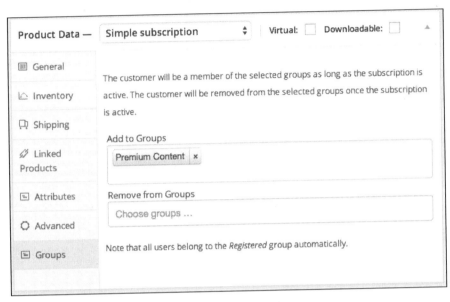

5. Click on **Update** to save the product.

 The product itself won't mention anything about the Group or the special privileges you added. The benefits of being a member should be typed in manually.

Creating a members-only store

To give your site a more exclusive feel, you could make it members only. You could show the products to anyone but only allow registered users to actually purchase them. You could then have an application form somewhere on your site that could collect their payment information. With a bit of magic from the **Catalog Visibility Options** plugin, you can easily control what types of users can see your products and how much information they see.

Getting ready

You must have the Catalog Visibility Options plugin (`http://www.woothemes.com/products/catalog-visibility-options/`) installed and activated on your site.

How to do it...

To create a members-only store, carry out the following steps:

1. From the WordPress admin, go to **WooCommerce | Settings**.
2. Click on the **Visibility Options** tab.
3. Change the **Purchases** setting to **Enabled for Logged In Users**.
4. Add a message in the **Alternate Content** field to direct the users to the application form on your site.

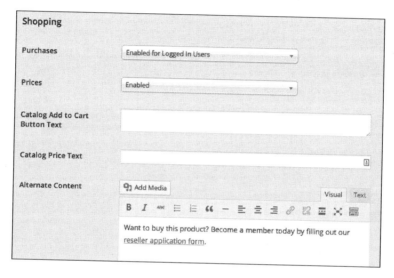

If you log out and go to the product page, you'll notice the absence of a purchase button and a message directing the user to the application form.

This book won't go into how to make contact forms in WordPress. One very flexible form-building plugin is **Ninja Forms**, available at WordPress.org for free. A simpler but slightly less powerful form plugin is the **Contact Form** module built into the Jetpack plugin, which is also available for free on WordPress.org.

Making subscription payments more consistent

One of the best parts about WooCommerce Subscriptions is that it runs on your own site. This means you can avoid a lot of fees that you would need to pay if you were to use other services. The downside to running it on your own site is that it uses the scheduling functionality built into WordPress, which relies on people visiting your site. If you don't have people visiting your site, then certain tasks won't happen. For large sites, this isn't a problem at all, but for smaller sites, you could have a subscription payment run a day late because no one visited the site the previous day.

With a few free tools, you can get around this issue by using services that ping your site every few minutes. That will ensure all of your subscription payments go off at the right time.

How to do it...

In order to make subscription payments more consistent, follow these steps:

1. From the WordPress admin, go to **Plugins | Add New**.
2. Run a search for the **Jetpack by WordPress.com** plugin.
3. Install and activate the plugin.
4. In the WordPress admin, you should see a notice asking you to **Connect to WordPress.com**.

Dashboard

Connect to WordPress.com

Your Jetpack is almost ready! Connect now to enable features like Stats, Likes, and Social Sharing.

5. Connect to WordPress.com. If you have an account, you only need to log in. If you don't have an account, you can create one for free and then log in.

   Now that we have Jetpack installed and connected to WordPress.com, we can use all of the features included in the plugin. The final thing we need to do is turn on the right Jetpack module.

6. Go to **Jetpack | Settings**.

7. Scroll down to **Monitor**, hover over it, and click on the **Activate** link.

How it works...

WordPress.com will check your site every few minutes, which will make sure any of your scheduled actions are on time. It will also send you an e-mail if you website ever goes down.

Customizing the subscription price string

If you're running a subscription site, there are bound to be things you want to customize to make your website reflect your brand. Subscriptions are loaded with hooks that developers can use to customize all sorts of things programmatically. We'll be manipulating the Subscriptions price string using a filter just to show how things are done.

Getting ready

You must have the WooCommerce Subscriptions plugin installed and activated on your site.

How to do it...

In order to customize the subscription price string, go through the following steps:

1. Open up your theme's `functions.php` file, located under `wp-content/themes/your-theme-name/`, or create a custom WooCommerce plugin and open up that file.

2. Add the following two lines of code. These tell Subscriptions to look for your modifications to the price string:

```
add_filter( 'woocommerce_subscriptions_price_string',
'woocommerce_cookbook_subscription_price_string', 10, 2 );
add_filter('woocommerce_subscriptions_product_price_string'
, 'woocommerce_cookbook_subscription_price_string', 10, 2
);
```

Now we need to write the modifications. Add the following code:

```
function woocommerce_cookbook_subscription_price_string(
$subscription_string, $product ) {
    $subscription_string = $subscription_string . '. In
2016 all subscriptions will get a price increase. Buy now
to be grandfathered in.';
    return $subscription_string;
}
```

3. Save and upload the file to your site.

Look at your subscription on the frontend and you can see the addition we made to the price string.

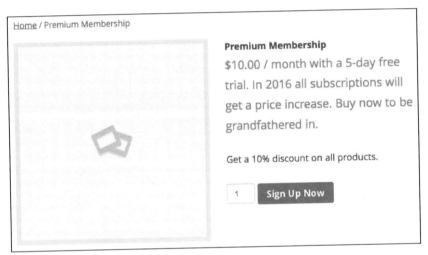

There's more...

There are dozens of filters you can use to modify all sorts of things in Subscriptions. If you're a developer, you can read through the developer docs at `http://docs.woothemes.com/document/subscriptions/develop/`.

Creating a custom subscription interval

The Subscriptions plugin already gives you the ability to create a day-long subscription, a month-long subscription, and subscriptions that can renew every other week. While it has a lot of intervals, it can't possibly have every one. If you want to have a subscription that renews every tenth week, you'll have to create a custom subscription interval. Using filters in Subscriptions, we can easily add this.

Getting ready

You must have the WooCommerce Subscriptions plugin installed and activated on your site. You should also have a subscription product already created.

How to do it...

In order to create a custom subscription interval, go through the following steps:

1. Open up your theme's `functions.php` file, located under `wp-content/themes/your-theme-name/`, or create a custom WooCommerce plugin and open up that file.

2. Add the following line of code. This tells Subscriptions to look for your modifications to the possible intervals:

   ```
   add_filter(
   'woocommerce_subscription_period_interval_strings',
   'woocommerce_cookbook_subscription_intervals' );
   ```

3. Now add the following code. This will actually add the extra intervals:

   ```
   function woocommerce_cookbook_subscription_intervals(
   $intervals ) {
       $intervals[10] = sprintf( __( 'every %s',
   'woocommerce-cookbook' ),
   WC_Subscriptions::append_numeral_suffix( 10 ) );
       return $intervals;
   }
   ```

 Note that there were two places where we put in our custom interval (10) in that string. If you want a different interval, then you should replace both instances of 10 with your desired number.

Now that we've created our custom interval, we need to edit our subscription product to use that interval.

1. In the WordPress admin, click on **Products** and navigate to your subscription product.

2. On the edit page, if you scroll down to the **Product Data** panel, you can now choose your custom interval.

3. Save your product and you're all done.

Exporting subscription orders

If you are using Subscriptions to manage all of the billing and you plan on using another system for some other part of your subscriptions, you will need to know who is an *active* subscriber. There are some plugins out there that do just this.

Getting ready

You must have the WooCommerce Subscriptions plugin installed and activated on your site. You should also have a subscription product already created.

You will also need to purchase and install the **WooCommerce Subscription Exporter** plugin from `http://codecanyon.net/item/woocommerce-subscription-exporter/6569668`.

How to do it...

To export subscription orders, perform the following steps:

1. From the WordPress admin, go to **WooCommerce | Subscriptions Export**.

2. Under **Subscriptions**, make sure **Active** is checked.

```
Selection

Select the data you want to export.

Subscriptions          (1)
  ✓  Active             (1)
     Pending           (0)
     Suspended         (0)
     Expired           (0)
     Cancelled         (0)
     Deleted           (0)
Start date
                                  Select the starting date of subscription start.
End date
                                  Select the end date of subscription start.
```

3. Click on **Calculate Export Size** and wait for the page to reload.
4. Then click on **Export**.
5. A CSV file will download that you can then upload into any other system.

There's more...

The default options for this plugin are quite useful and most likely don't need to be changed. However, if you need special formatting for your CSV file, you can manipulate all sorts of settings by going to **WooCommerce | Subscriptions Export | Options**.

You can do a lot with the WooCommerce Subscription Exporter extension—more than just exporting active subscribers. You could also run a report that lists all users who cancelled their subscription in the past three months. You could get all of their e-mails and ask them why they left. Exporting active subscribers is really just the beginning.

5
Setting Up Shipping Methods

In this chapter, we will cover:

- ▸ Setting a minimum order amount to unlock free shipping
- ▸ Configuring Flat Rate Shipping
- ▸ Creating shipping classes
- ▸ Getting live shipping quotes with USPS
- ▸ Creating a table of shipping rates with Table Rate Shipping
- ▸ Allowing shipping only to the continental US
- ▸ Enabling free shipping on a per product basis
- ▸ Tracking your shipments with Shipment Tracking
- ▸ Exporting orders for fulfillment to ShipStation

Introduction

WooCommerce has some pretty smart defaults so you actually could start selling products right now. If you're a new store owner, that's actually not a bad thing. Setting up shipping methods can be quite complex and frustrating, which is why I always recommend starting with simple shipping methods and gradually exploring more complex methods.

The first two recipes deal with the default WooCommerce shipping options and give you a ton of functionality right out of the box. **Flat Rate Shipping** is quite configurable and can handle many different shipping options while still being relatively simple to set up. **Free shipping** is also quite easy to set up and you can entice users to buy more products by offering free shipping for a certain order total.

If you have very complex shipping instructions for your products we'll be covering **Table Rate Shipping**, which can handle just about any type of shipping rule whether it's calculated by weight, price, quantity, or type of item. It's the ultimate Swiss army knife of shipping. We'll also cover getting live shipping quotes from USPS and some extra tricks that certain stores might need.

Setting a minimum order amount to unlock free shipping

Free shipping is something that users are beginning to expect in the online world. You don't have to have it available for every order but there should be someway to unlock it. Built into WooCommerce is a Free Shipping method that can be configured to unlock after a specified order total has been reached or when the customer has a special coupon. We'll be setting the Free Shipping method to unlock after a customer has $100 of product(s) in their cart. With a little marketing on your site customers will be shooting for $100 even if they don't need that much.

How to do it...

In order to set a minimum order amount to unlock free shipping, go through the following steps:

1. From the WordPress admin, go to **WooCommerce | Settings | Shipping**. From here you can access all of the WooCommerce **Shipping Options**.

2. Make sure that both **Enable shipping** and **Enable the shipping calculator on the cart page** are checked:

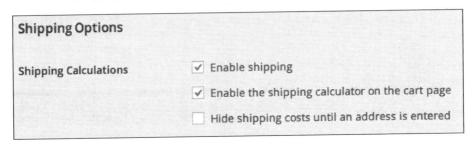

3. Click on **Free Shipping**.

4. Make sure **Enable Free Shipping** is checked.

5. For the **Free Shipping Requires...** setting, select **A minimum order amount (defined below)**. In the **Minimum Order Amount** field enter your minimum order amount to unlock free shipping:

Free Shipping Requires...	A minimum order amount (defined below) ⬍
Minimum Order Amount ⓘ	100

6. Click on **Save changes** and you're done.

There's more...

If you have Free Shipping as the only shipping method for your store then users who purchase less than $100 of physical products won't be able to checkout. You must enable some other shipping method for those users. In the next recipe we'll look at configuring Flat Rate Shipping, which is one of the more simple shipping methods to set up. Before setting up any other shipping methods I highly recommend you look into Flat Rate Shipping.

Configuring Flat Rate Shipping

While free shipping is great, not all stores can have the markup required to give away free shipping to all orders. You could connect to a shipping service and get live quotes from them but that takes extra work getting an account and making sure all of your products have weights and dimensions. An easier option is to set up **Flat Rate Shipping**, which gives you the option of estimating costs by providing a per-order cost with an additional per item cost. For many stores this is good enough and even for stores that want to have more complex options, it's good to try out the basic options first.

Getting ready

Make sure shipping is enabled on your site. See the *Setting a minimum order amount to unlock free shipping* recipe in this chapter to see how this is done.

How to do it...

In order to configure Flat Rate Shipping, have a look at the following steps:

1. From the WordPress admin, go to **WooCommerce | Settings | Shipping**.
2. Click on **Flat Rate**.

3. Check the **Enable this shipping method** setting.

4. We're going to add a per-order cost that should cover most of our shipping costs. In our case we're going to have a per-order cost of $8. Set the **Cost per order** setting to **8**.

   This works great for people who order a small handful of items. However, some users will order dozens or hundreds of items. We want to take those cases into account.

5. Under the **Additional Costs** section set the **Costs Added...** dropdown to **Per Item - charge shipping for each item individually**.

   In the **Costs** table right beneath that setting, we need to add a cost per item.

6. Under the **Cost** column add a per item price of **2**:

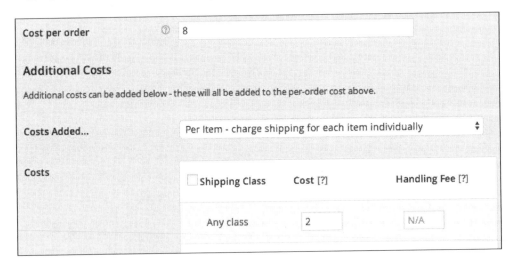

7. Click on **Save changes**.

   At this point, you have a pretty solid Flat Rate Shipping method. We're going to take it one step further by presenting users with a flat rate as well as an express shipping rate, where we charge users a premium for the **rush** service.

8. Under **Add-on Rates**, you can add an additional rate by setting this: **Enter Rush Order | 15 | order**. This should give the user the option of upgrading to a rush service for an extra $15 when choosing shipping options. Have a look at the following demonstrative screenshot:

Cart Totals

CART SUBTOTAL	$40.00
SHIPPING AND HANDLING	⦿ Flat Rate: **$16.00** ◯ Rush Order: **$31.00**
ORDER TOTAL	$56.00

Proceed to Checkout

There's more...

There are tons of extra options here that we haven't touched. If you have items of different sizes, you may add a per-item cost based on the shipping class of an item. Go through the following recipe to create shipping classes.

Creating shipping classes

Most stores will have a couple of products that are different in size, shape, or weight from the rest of the products, and trying to create one set of rules for all of your products can be a bit tricky. You might end up not estimating enough for some orders and estimating too much for other orders. Neither one is good for your business.

To help store owners, WooCommerce has shipping classes that allow you to group your products. With multiple groups you can create different shipping rules for each group, which will give you much more accurate shipping estimates. These shipping classes are used throughout WooCommerce. They're used in Flat Rate Shipping (which is included in WooCommerce) and some of the WooCommerce extensions like Table Rate Shipping.

Getting ready

Make sure you already have at least one product in your store.

How to do it...

The first thing we have to do is create our shipping classes by performing the following steps:

1. From the WordPress admin, go to **Products | Shipping** Classes.

2. Fill out the **Name** field.

3. Optionally fill out the **Slug**, **Parent**, and **Description** fields. These aren't used by WooCommerce unless you're doing custom coding.

4. Click on **Add New Shipping Class**.

   We've created one shipping class. Repeat this for as many shipping classes you need. Once you're done creating shipping classes, we have to add them to our products.

5. In the main WordPress menu, click on **Products** and then navigate to one of your products.

6. Scroll down to the **Product Data** tab.

7. Click on the **Shipping** tab.

8. Select the class from the **Shipping Class** dropdown.

There's more...

Your product now has a shipping class. This won't change anything until you add special rules for that shipping class. You can do that in Flat Rate Shipping, Table Rate Shipping, and more.

Getting live shipping quotes with USPS

If you want to give users the exact shipping cost and not have to figure out how to do it with Flat Rate Shipping, you can get rates directly from **USPS**. That way, you can't estimate the costs wrong and lose money on shipping. It takes a bit of extra work to set it up, but the results make it very easy for users to select the exact shipping method they want and there's no confusion for the admin.

You could also get rates from UPS or FedEx and the process is very similar. The reason I choose to use USPS is because it's slightly easier to set up. With USPS, WooThemes has been able to include credentials in the plugin, which means you have one less account to set up.

Getting ready

Make sure shipping is enabled on your site. See the *Setting a minimum order amount to unlock free shipping* recipe in this chapter to see how this is done. You'll need to have weights and dimensions for all of your products. If they don't have both weight and dimensions set, you won't get any results. You'll also need the **WooCommerce USPS** plugin (available on WooThemes.com) installed and activated on your site.

How to do it...

In order to get live shipping quotes with USPS, go through the following steps:

1. From the WordPress admin, go to **WooCommerce | Settings | Shipping**.
2. Click on **USPS**.
3. Enable the shipping method by checking the **Enable this shipping method** setting.
4. Enter your zip code in the **Origin Postcode** field.
5. Make sure the **Flat Rate Boxes & envelopes** dropdown is set to **Yes – Enable flat rate services**:

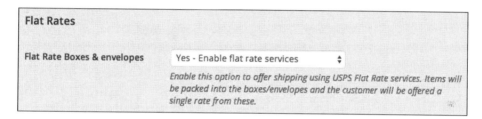

6. Click on **Save changes**.

At this point, if you go to the frontend of your site and add a few products to your cart, you should see some quotes from USPS based on how many products you have and how many can fit into each flat rate box. Let's take a look at the following screenshot that displays some details about Cart Totals:

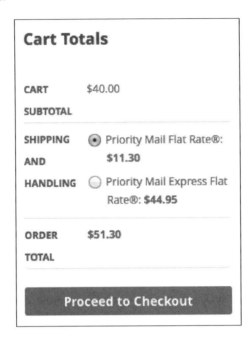

 Naturally, you may see different rates from what's shown in the preceding screenshot. It all depends on the size, dimensions, weight, and quantity of products you have in your cart.

Getting this far enables you to use the flat rate boxes from USPS, which is convenient for many businesses. However, some businesses want or need to have custom box sizes. You can enter your own box sizes and USPS will give you a custom quote for using your custom boxes. For entering custom box sizes, you need to perform following steps:

1. Under **API Rates**, check the **Enable Standard Services from the API** setting. Some new fields will appear.

2. For the **Parcel Packing Method** setting, select **Recommended: Pack into boxes with weights and dimensions**.

3. Now add your custom box sizes. You can add as many as you need by clicking on the **Add Box** button as shown in the following screenshot:

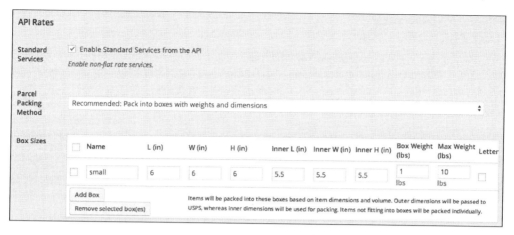

	Name	L (in)	W (in)	H (in)	Inner L (in)	Inner W (in)	Inner H (in)	Box Weight (lbs)	Max Weight (lbs)	Letter
☐	small	6	6	6	5.5	5.5	5.5	1 lbs	10 lbs	☐

Add Box

Remove selected box(es)

Items will be packed into these boxes based on item dimensions and volume. Outer dimensions will be passed to USPS, whereas inner dimensions will be used for packing. Items not fitting into boxes will be packed individually.

4. Press **Save changes** to make sure everything is saved.

On the frontend, you should now see different rates. Have a look at the following demonstrative screenshot:

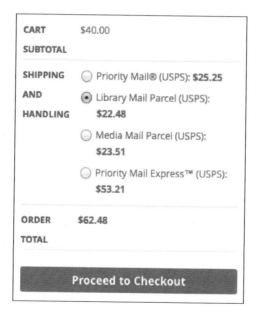

> If you're having trouble getting rates, make sure that all of your products have weights and dimensions set on the **Edit Product** page on the **Shipping** tab of the **Product Data** panel. Then make sure they can fit into at least one box. Then make sure you have a destination set on the **Cart** page. You can set a destination by clicking on the **Calculate Shipping** link.

How it works...

The USPS plugin includes a **box packer**. This box packer will automatically figure out how many items can fit in a box and then send the list of boxes to USPS. USPS does all of the rate calculation on their side and returns the results to WooCommerce, which are then displayed for the customer.

Creating a table of shipping rates with Table Rate Shipping

Getting live rates works very well for shipping small- to medium-sized packages. It doesn't work very well when you want to ship something large such as furniture or something heavy such as sand. You'll most likely have to contract a shipping provider that doesn't have a plugin and you'll have to create your own rates. That is exactly why Table Rate Shipping exists—for such custom scenarios.

One of the things Table Rate Shipping is very good at is having different pricing rules for different geographic regions. If you deliver furniture you most likely have a rate for local delivery, another rate for delivery in the state, another rate for out-of-state purchases, and a rate for international sales. These can be very easily set up with Table Rate Shipping.

Getting ready

Make sure shipping is enabled on your site. See the *Setting a minimum order amount to unlock free shipping* recipe in this chapter to see how that is done. You'll need to have weights set for all of your products. You'll also need the WooCommerce Table Rate Shipping plugin (available on WooThemes.com) installed and activated on your site.

How to do it...

The first thing we need to do is create zones for the different areas we're delivering to. For creating **Shipping Zones**, we need to perform the following steps:

1. From the WordPress admin, go to **WooCommerce | Shipping Zones**.

   There's a default zone, which we'll leave in place. We can configure that default zone with pricing rules later. First, we need to create the rest of the zones.

2. Enter a **Zone Name**.

3. Under **Type of zone**, select **This shipping zone is based on one or more countries**.

4. Start typing United States in the country box and select the correct suggestion:

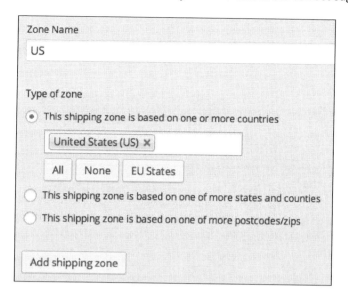

5. Click on **Add shipping zone**.

   We need to create two more zones. One based on the state and the other based on the zip code. I'll be using Denver, Colorado, as an example.

6. For the state, you need to repeat the process we gone through earlier along with making sure you select **This shipping zone is based on one of more states and counties** for the **Type of zone** setting and then type in your state name.

7. For deliveries in your city, it's best to work with zip codes. Make sure you select **This shipping zone is based on one of more postcodes/zips** for the **Type of zone** setting. You can easily target multiple zip codes by using ranges or wildcards. For example, 80201-80209 or 8020*.

   Now that we've created all of our shipping zones, it's time to configure them with rates.

8. Start with any zone you like, hover over the name of the zone, and click on **Configure shipping method**:

9. Add a new table of rates to that zone by selecting **Table rates** and then clicking on **Add To Zone**:

10. Click on the title of the table of rates to edit it.

    With furniture being all sorts of different sizes, we're going to use weight to come up with a cost.

11. Leave **Calculation Type** as **Per order**.

12. Click on **+ Add Shipping Rate**.

13. Fill in the rate. In our case, we're going to create three different tiers: 0-100lbs, 101-300 lbs, and 301+ lbs, all with different prices. In the following screenshot, we will fill rates as per these three tiers:

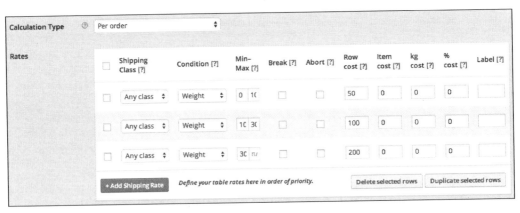

14. Click **Save shipping Method** when you're done.

15. Repeat this for each zone.

That's a lot of work but we've created some very custom shipping rates based on weight and destination.

There's more...

There's a lot in Table Rate Shipping. We could write a whole chapter on the many different ways you can use Table Rate Shipping but that's not the best use of space. To see some more examples on the official documentation page refer to `http://docs.woothemes.com/document/table-rate-shipping-v2/`.

Allowing shipping only to the continental US

Shipping to Alaska and Hawaii is very different from shipping to the rest of the continental United States. The rates and time to deliver are much higher. You may want to disable some or all shipping methods from shipping to those states. You could do this with Table Rate Shipping but if you don't want to purchase that extension you could write a bit of code that does the same thing.

Getting ready

Make sure shipping is enabled on your site. See the **Setting a minimum order amount to unlock free shipping** recipe in this chapter to see how this is done.

How to do it...

In order to only allow shipping to the continental US, let's go through the following steps:

1. Open up your theme's `functions.php` file, which is located at `wp-content/themes/your-theme-name/`, or a custom WooCommerce plugin in your code editor. Paste the following code at the bottom of the file:

    ```
    function woocommerce_cookbook_only_ship_to_continental_us(
    $available_methods ) {
        global $woocommerce;
        $excluded_states = array( 'AK','HI','GU','PR' );
        if ( in_array(
    $woocommerce->customer->get_shipping_state(),
    $excluded_states ) ) {
            // Empty the $available_methods array
            $available_methods = array();
        }
        return $available_methods;
    }
    add_filter( 'woocommerce_package_rates',
    woocommerce_cookbook_only_ship_to_continental_us, 10 );
    ```

2. Save and upload that file.

How it works...

When WooCommerce is calculating rates, we add some extra logic to determine whether the shipping methods are valid. We create an array of states, and if the shipping address has one of the states in the array, then we return a list with no valid shipping methods. If the shipping address doesn't have one of the states mentioned, we do not do anything and return the list of states that was sent to this function.

There's more...

This code snippet prevents all shipping methods from working. You could write additional logic using the `$available_methods` array to only remove certain shipping methods. You could, for example, only offer free shipping to the continental US and offer USPS quotes anywhere in the US.

Enabling free shipping on a per product basis

The Free Shipping method that comes with WooCommerce is pretty flexible. What it's not great at is allowing a store to mark one or two items to use free shipping for and leave the rest of the products to use your other shipping methods. We can use the shipping classes built into WooCommerce combined with a little bit of code to mark any number of products eligible for free shipping.

Getting ready

Make sure you have the free shipping method enabled on your site.

How to do it...

In order to enable free shipping on a per product basis, go through the following steps:

1. The first step is to create the shipping class we're going to use to mark items eligible for free shipping. If you don't know how to create shipping classes, see the *Creating shipping classes* recipe in this chapter.

    Once you have a shipping class, you need to copy the shipping class **Slug**, which we can use to identify that shipping class in the code.

2. On the right-hand side of the **Shipping Classes** page you should see a list of shipping classes. Copy the **Slug** for the shipping class you just copied. The following screenshot shows the Shipping Classes section:

Name	Description	Slug	Count
Free Shipping		free-shipping	0

    Now that we have our shipping class, we can write the code to add some extra functionality for that shipping class.

3. Add the following code to your theme's `functions.php` file, which is located at `wp-content/themes/your-theme-name/` or a custom WooCommerce plugin:

```php
/*
 * Enable free shipping for orders with products that have the
free-shipping shipping class slug
 *
 * @param bool $is_available
 */
function woocommerce_cookbook_enable_free_shipping (
$is_available ) {
    global $woocommerce;
    // set the shipping classes that are eligible
    $eligible = array( 'free-shipping' );
    // get cart contents
    $cart_items = $woocommerce->cart->get_cart();
    // make sure there is something in the cart
    if ( is_array( $cart_items ) && count( $cart_items ) >1
) {
        // loop through the items checking to make sure
they all have the right class
        foreach ( $cart_items as $key => $item ) {
            if ( ! in_array( $item['data']->shipping_class,
$eligible ) ) {
                // this item doesn't have the right class.
return false
                return false;
            }
        }
    }
    // nothing out of the ordinary return the default value
    return $is_available;
}
add_filter(
'woocommerce_shipping_free_shipping_is_available',
'woocommerce_cookbook_enable_free_shipping', 20 );
```

That's it! That's all the code you'll need. The last thing we need to do is add the shipping class to our products, as shown in the following screenshot. This is explained in detail in the *Creating shipping classes* recipe of this chapter.

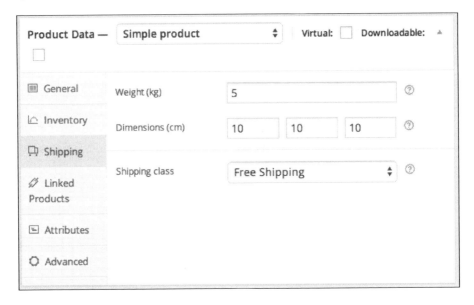

How it works...

This code snippet works a bit counter-intuitively. It doesn't automatically let any product with the shipping class use free shipping. It instead prevents every other product from using free shipping. The advantage of this is that there's very little code and you can still use the free shipping settings. You could, for example, require that the user purchase $5 of goods before unlocking free shipping for your tiny items.

Tracking your shipments with Shipment Tracking

It's a common practice to give the user a tracking number for their shipments. In addition to being a nice experience for the customer, it's also good for store owners because you'll have less follow-up e-mails asking where their package is. A customer can click on a link in their confirmation e-mails and see exactly where it is.

Getting ready

If you have an order awaiting fulfillment in your store you don't need to do anything. If you don't have an order in your store, it's best to create a test order using the **Cheque Payment** gateway so you don't have to spend any money.

You'll also need the WooCommerce Shipment Tracking plugin, available at WooThemes.com, installed and activated on your site.

How to do it...

To track your shipments with Shipment Tracking, take a look at the following steps:

1. From the WordPress admin, go to **WooCommerce | Orders**.

2. Navigate to an order that needs fulfillment and click on it to go to the **Order Detail** page.

3. On the **Order Detail** page, you'll see a **Shipment Tracking** box.

4. Enter data in **Provider**, **Tracking number**, and the **Date shipped** boxes. The more information you put in here, the more useful it will be for your customer:

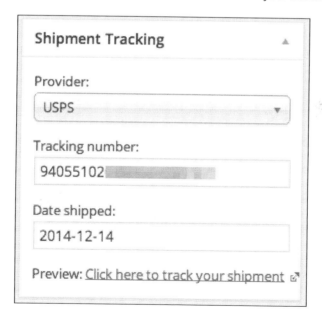

5. Click on **Save Order**. This will save the order and refresh the page.

6. Now change **Order status** to **Completed**:

7. Click on **Save Order**. This will save the order and send out the order completed e-mail.

8. The customer will see when their order was sent out with a link to get updates:

There's more...

The Shipment Tracking extension works with dozens of providers all around the world and is the best solution. If you use USPS, there's a complimentary plugin that makes the whole process easier. The Stamps.com API extension available at WooThemes.com will allow you to get the tracking number from the WooCommerce order screen and is a huge time-saver.

Exporting orders for fulfillment to ShipStation

If you only have one store, then it's pretty easy to manage all of the orders from within WooCommerce. If you have multiple WooCommerce stores or you sell items on EBay or some other e-commerce platform, then it's worth exporting the orders out of all of the stores into one place where you can manage them. One of the best tools to do this is ShipStation.

Getting ready

You must install and activate the free ShipStation plugin from WooThemes.com.

ShipStation only works when it can talk to your site, so it must be accessible online. You can't use a test site that's running on your local machine.

How to do it...

Getting your store to export orders is pretty painless. You need to copy a key from WooCommerce into your ShipStation account. The first part of this is getting that key from WooCommerce.

1. From the WordPress admin, go to **WooCommerce | Settings | Integrations**.

2. If this is the only plugin that adds an integration, the ShipStation page will be loaded automatically. If it's not loaded automatically, click on **ShipStation**.

3. Copy **Authentication Key**. You'll need it during the ShipStation setup:

Now you'll have to set up your ShipStation account.

4. Go through their setup process. You'll have to create an account, validate the e-mail address you entered, and then set up your store.

5. Add a new store to your ShipStation account. You'll need to enter your store's URL and your **Auth Key**, as shown in the following screenshot:

Woo COMMERCE

Your WooCommerce store can be integrated with ShipStation in just minutes. To grant ShipStation access to your WooCommerce web site, please follow the instructions below. Additional detailed instructions can be found in the Marketplaces section of our Help Website. **Please note this plug-in requires the use of WooCommerce 2.2+.**

1. Dowload the ShipStation Integration plug-in to your computer.
2. In your Wordpress Admin dashboard, navigate to **Plugins > Add New**. Here, click on the **Upload** link and select the plug-in zip file from your local computer and then click **Install Now**.
3. Activate the new extension by clicking the link on the installation page or through the **Plugins** menu in WordPress.
4. Within your Wordpress Admin dashboard, navigate to the **WooCommerce** menu, then **Settings > Integration**.
5. Copy the **Authentication Key** from WooCommerce and paste it into the **Auth Key** field below.
6. Enter your WordPress site's domain (e.g., http://yoursite.com) into the **Store URL** field below.
7. Within WooCommerce, choose which order statuses to export to ShipStation and map these statuses by placing them in the relevant fields below. When finished, click **Save Changes** in WooCommerce.
8. Click **Test Connection** to see if the steps you followed worked correctly.
9. Click on **Finish** to make this store active in ShipStation!

Auth Key

WCSS-87e2cc953b11c3359cf3

Store URL

http://example.com/

Test Connection

6. Click on **Finish** and you're done.

When you start using ShipStation, you'll want to set up a few shipping providers to get quotes through ShipStation and create shipping labels.

How it works...

The default settings for this plugin are pretty useful. By default, any processing— completed, on-hold, or cancelled orders—are sent to ShipStation. You can manage those orders in ShipStation, and once they've been marked as completed, they'll also be marked as completed in WooCommerce.

There's more...

This extension integrates very nicely with WooCommerce Shipment Tracker. If you mark an order as completed in ShipStation, it will also be marked as completed in WooCommerce. The shipping provider's name and tracking number will be automatically filled out and sent to the customer.

6
Getting Paid

In this chapter, we will cover:

- ▸ Configuring the PayPal gateway
- ▸ Configuring the Simplify Commerce gateway
- ▸ Configuring the Stripe gateway
- ▸ Enabling HTTPS on checkout
- ▸ Enabling HTTPS on specific pages
- ▸ Tracking e-commerce transactions with Google Analytics
- ▸ Creating an invoice
- ▸ Adding a fee per gateway using the Payment Gateway based Fees extension

Introduction

By default, you can only accept checks, which is, let's be honest, not very useful. Most e-commerce stores don't accept bank transfers or checks. The joy of e-commerce is receiving instant payment and fulfilling the order that very day.

The first three recipes in this chapter show you how to—set up three different payment gateways, all of which allow you to accept payment on the spot. They all do it in slightly different ways, and you may want to set up multiple options for your store. The first two gateways are included in WooCommerce. The third recipe is for Stripe, which has a very good reputation on the Web, it requires an extension from WooThemes.com.

Once you get payment options set up on your store, you may want to do a few more things. Adding **Secure Sockets Layer** (**SSL**) to your site will make it more secure, tracking e-commerce transactions will make your Google Analytics reports more useful, and you can even add fees to certain gateways so that you can encourage users to use a particular gateway.

Configuring the PayPal gateway

PayPal is a place where people who frequently spend money online can park their money until they need to spend it. Accepting money online via PayPal is very common, and some users prefer to spend money on PayPal rather than share their credit card details with an unknown site. PayPal can also work for people who don't have a PayPal account and want to use a credit card.

Getting ready

You need to sign up for a PayPal account at `https://www.paypal.com/signup/account`.

How to do it...

There are quite a few steps to setting up PayPal. Luckily, not all of them are required. The first part will allow you to capture payments immediately. In order to configure the PayPal gateway, go through the following steps:

1. From the WordPress admin, go to **WooCommerce | Settings | Checkout**. From here, you can access all of the WooCommerce payment options.

2. Click on **PayPal**.

3. Check **Enable PayPal standard**:

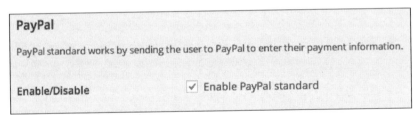

4. You must fill out the **PayPal Email** field.

5. Scroll down and click on Save changes.

 You can check the **Debug Log** field. It can be very hard to find errors that happen on transactions using PayPal without the logs; having the PayPal logs available will save a lot of time in trying to diagnose what's causing the transaction to fail.

At this point, you can capture payments. With a few extra settings filled in, you can process refunds from within WooCommerce, which is a big time saver.

6. Scroll down to **API Credentials**:

API Credentials

Enter your PayPal API credentials to process refunds via PayPal. Learn how to access your PayPal API Credentials here.

API Username	⑦	Optional

API Password	⑦	Optional

API Signature	⑦	Optional

7. Follow the link to the PayPal website to get your API information.

8. Fill out **API Username**, **API Password**, and **API Signature**.

9. Click on **Save changes**.

 Some web hosts have problems with the way PayPal notifies the store of a successful transaction, which is called **Instant Payment Notification** (**IPN**). If you are seeing a payment marked as complete in PayPal but not in WooCommerce, then you can fill in the **PayPal Identity Token** field. This will allow PayPal to use a different protocol for notifying your site.

There's more...

There are some people who will only use PayPal and others who refuse to use PayPal altogether. Many stores handle this by providing PayPal as well as one other gateway to handle credit cards.

The PayPal gateway included in WooCommerce is known as PayPal standard. Note, however, that it doesn't include the advanced functionality included with some PayPal business accounts. If you need that functionality, there are several PayPal extensions available on WooThemes.com.

Configuring the Simplify Commerce gateway

In WooCommerce 2.2, the Simplify Commerce gateway was added to WooCommerce. This is huge news, because Simplify Commerce is a really user-friendly gateway and it processes credit cards without taking you to another site (unlike PayPal). Simplify Commerce is pretty easy to set up and doesn't require a merchant account as some older processors do. If you're just getting started, Simplify Commerce is an excellent payment gateway to use.

Simplify Commerce is only available to merchants in the United States. If your store location is set to another country, you won't see the gateway.

Getting ready

An SSL certificate is required to process actual credit cards. Contact your host about setting one up on your site. You don't need an SSL certificate for testing.

There are some other technical hardware requirements listed at `http://docs.woothemes.com/document/simplify-commerce/`.

How to do it...

In order to configure the Simplify Commerce gateway, go through the following steps:

1. From the WordPress admin, go to **WooCommerce | Settings | Checkout**.

2. Click on **Simplify Commerce**.

 You'll see a banner encouraging you to sign up for Simplify Commerce. I recommend signing up via this banner. As of this writing, Simplify Commerce has a promotion giving you $10,000 of transactions with no fees if you sign up via the banner.

Getting started

Simplify Commerce is your merchant account and payment gateway all rolled into one. Choose Simplify Commerce as your WooCommerce payment gateway to get access to your money quickly with a powerful, secure payment engine backed by MasterCard.

Sign up for Simplify Commerce   Learn more

3. Check the **Enable Simplify Commerce** field.

4. Fill out the **Public Key** and **Private Key** fields.

5. Click on **Save changes**.

   At this point, you can charge credit cards. It's advisable to do a few test orders. To do those, you'll need to enter your sandbox API credentials.

6. Check the **Enable Sandbox Mode** setting. Note that the **Public Key** and **Private Key** fields are replaced with **Sandbox Public Key** and **Sandbox Private Key**.

7. Fill out the **Sandbox Public Key** and **Sandbox Private Key** fields.

8. Click on **Save changes**.

> By default, the **Description** field will say something like **Pay with your credit card via Simplify Commerce by Mastercard**. I suggest simplifying this to *Pay with your credit card*. Most customers don't know or care what Simplify Commerce is. They just know that they want to pay with their credit card.

Configuring the Stripe gateway

Stripe is a modern payment processor that combines a traditional payment gateway and merchant account into one service. That makes it possible to set up the gateway in a matter of minutes. The ease of setup along with simple pricing and a well-documented API has made Stripe one of the most popular gateways for web developers.

Getting ready

It's best to open a Stripe account before reading or going through this recipe. You'll need to enter your important business details like business tax ID number if you're in the US. You'll also need the WooCommerce Stripe plugin (available on WooThemes.com) installed and activated on your site.

An SSL certificate is required to process actual credit cards. Contact your host about setting one up on your site. You don't need an SSL certificate to set up the plugin or test.

How to do it...

In order to configure the Stripe gateway, let's take a look at the following steps:

1. From the WordPress admin, go to **WooCommerce | Settings | Checkout**.

2. Click on **Stripe**.

3. Check the **Enable Stripe** field.

By default, the **Title** and **Description** field will say something like **Pay with your credit card via Stripe**. I suggest simplifying this to *Pay with your credit card*. Most customers don't know or care what Stripe is. They just know that they want to pay with their credit card.

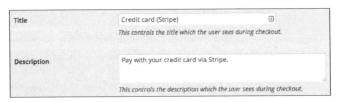

Title	Credit card (Stripe)
	This controls the title which the user sees during checkout.
Description	Pay with your credit card via Stripe.
	This controls the description which the user sees during checkout.

4. Log in to your Stripe account and copy your **Live Secret Key**, **Live Publishable Key**, **Test Secret Key**, and **Test Publishable Key** into the corresponding fields in WooCommerce. You can also go straight to the API keys in your Stripe account via `https://dashboard.stripe.com/account/apikeys`.

If you usually ship your products a day after receiving the order, I recommend leaving the **Capture charge immediately** setting checked. If it takes you a few days, then I recommend unchecking that field and manually charging the customer when you ship the product. You should technically only charge the customer once the order has shipped, but it's most likely not worth the hassle if you ship the product within 24 hours.

5. Click on the **Save changes** button.

To make checking out a bit easier for your customers, it's nice to *remember* their credit card number. You can do that by checking the **Enable saved cards** field. WooCommerce never stores credit card numbers, but it can remember credit card tokens, which is something that a gateway will send to WooCommerce after a transaction. It's something only your Stripe account can use for further orders, and if someone hacks your site there's no chance of them getting the credit card number. This means you don't have to worry about PCI compliance.

There's more...

With Stripe, you need an SSL certificate and you'll have to protect your checkout page. In the following recipe, we'll show you how to do that.

Enabling HTTPS on checkout

If you're using a payment gateway that has the users enter their credit card number on your site, you'll need an SSL certificate installed on your site and you'll have to enable HTTPS on your site to protect your visitors' information.

Official WooThemes.com payment gateways that should use an SSL certificate will not work without one. This is a good thing, because you can't set it up wrong and then be liable for stolen credit card numbers.

There are some payment gateways that look like you're entering a credit card number on your site, but they might be using technology to embed a secure page within your site. If you're using a WooThemes plugin, don't worry about it. All of those plugins have been audited and are secure. If they require an SSL certificate, they will be clearly documented.

If you're using a plugin from a third party, it's worth checking with the developers to make sure everything is secure.

Getting ready

Before you can enable HTTPS on any page, you need to have an SSL certificate installed on your site. You can contact your host to help you with this.

How to do it...

In order to enable HTTPS on checkout, refer to the following steps:

1. From the WordPress admin, go to **WooCommerce | Settings | Checkout**.
2. Check the **Force secure checkout** setting:

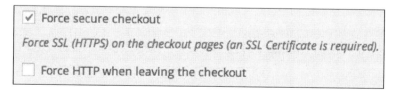

Checking the **Force secure checkout** setting will make the **Force HTTP when leaving the checkout** setting appear. You can enable this setting if you like, but there's not much of a gain to force people to use HTTP on other pages. It could also conflict with another plugin. I recommend leaving this setting off.

3. Click on **Save changes**.

There's more...

Users entering credit cards isn't the only time you should use HTTPS. It's also recommended to put it on any page with a password or other sensitive information. For that reason, it's worth using additional plugins to secure login pages. We'll cover that in the next recipe.

Enabling HTTPS on specific pages

Whenever users enter sensitive information, you should protect that information by making the page secure (HTTPS). This information could be credit card details, passwords, health information, or personal information such as social security numbers. By using HTTPS, you prevent other people from reading the communication between your website and the end user.

One of the pages automatically created when you install WooCommerce pages is a **My Account** page. Since users could enter a password on that page, it's worth securing that page.

Getting ready

Before you can enable HTTPS on any page, you need to have an SSL certificate installed on your site. You can contact your host to help you with this.

How to do it...

There's an easy-to-use plugin to help us with this. We'll have to install the plugin and then configure it to protect pages on our site by performing the following steps:

1. In the WordPress admin, click on the **Plugins** menu and then click on **Add New**.
2. Search for the **WordPress HTTPS** plugin.
3. Install and activate the plugin.

   You should now see a new menu in the WordPress admin called **HTTPS**. We need to perform a certain action on the frontend of our site and then we will be ready to use those new settings.

4. Go to the frontend of your site and navigate to the **My Account** page. It should have been automatically created with the rest of the WooCommerce pages.

5. Copy the URL of the page, as shown in the following screenshot:

6. Go back to the WordPress admin.

7. Click on the **HTTPS** menu.

8. Paste the URL in the **URL Filters** meta box, as shown in the following screenshot:

At this point, we've protected the **My Account** page. You can repeat this process for any other pages where you ask the user for sensitive information.

9. Click on **Save Changes**.

If you go to the frontend of your site, you should be able to go to the **My Account** page and it should automatically load in HTTPS.

There's more...

There's another login page we haven't yet protected. It's worth protecting your main admin page. You can do this by enabling the **Force SSL Administration** setting in the **General Settings** panel on the settings page of **HTTPS**:

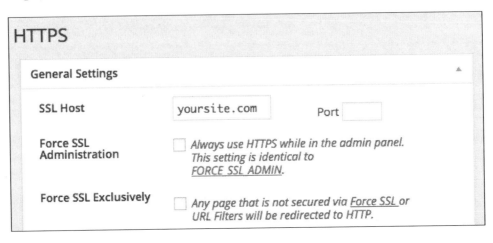

Tracking e-commerce transactions with Google Analytics

If you're building your first e-commerce store, you might think that getting a lot of traffic to your site is always good. While traffic is usually good, it helps if you can figure out whether your traffic is actually buying. When you send e-commerce data to Google Analytics, you can figure out exactly which traffic is buying. You could see that users from Facebook typically spend $5–10 whereas users who come from your newsletter spend $50–100. Now that you have the numbers, you can make more informed decisions.

This is one of the steps that I recommend for every single e-commerce store. Even if you don't plan on using the data, it will only take a few minutes to set up. Moreover, if you decide you want to use the data down the line, you will have a huge backlog of data.

Getting ready

You should already have a free Google Analytics account set up for your website. You should also be using a plugin to send your non-e-commerce traffic data to Google Analytics. A good plugin to do that is Google Analytics by Yoast.

How to do it...

The ability to track Google Analytics data used to be included in WooCommerce, until WooCommerce 2.1. At that point, the functionality was put into a free plugin for the ease of updating both WooCommerce and the Google Analytics Integration plugin. We need to install that plugin and then configure a few settings.

1. In the WordPress admin, click on the **Plugins** menu and then click on **Add New**.

2. Look for the `WooCommerce Google Analytics Integration` plugin.

3. Install and activate the plugin.

   There is one setting we need to configure in your Google Analytics account. You need to enable **E-Commerce tracking**. It should take a few clicks to enable the setting. You can follow their official instructions at `https://support.google.com/analytics/answer/1009612?hl=en`.

   Alright, we've got the plugin installed—your Google Analytics account is configured and ready. We just need to check a few boxes to send the right data to Google Analytics.

4. From the WordPress admin, go to **WooCommerce | Settings | Integration**.

   If this is the only integration you've added, then Google Analytics Integration will pop up. If you've added multiple integrations, you'll have to click on **Google Analytics**.

5. Fill out your **Google Analytics ID**. You can find your Google Analytics ID in Google Analytics under your list of sites, as shown in the following screenshot:

6. Make sure you leave **Add tracking code** to your site unchecked.

You could use this plugin for all Google Analytics tracking, but other plugins have more options. I always advise people to use a separate plugin like Google Analytics by Yoast for tracking non-e-commerce data.

7. It's advisable to use the new Universal Analytics features rather than the classic features. If you have an older Google Analytics account, you'll have to first convert your account to a Universal account and then check the Use Universal Analytics setting instead of Classic Google Analytics setting. If you created an account mid-2014 or later, it should already use Universal Analytics.

8. Check the **Add eCommerce tracking code to the thankyou page** setting.

9. Click on **Save changes**.

There's more...

With Universal Analytics, there's a new feature called Enhanced E-Commerce, which gives you more data you can use. This feature is on the roadmap for the Google Analytics plugin and should be completed in early 2015. Once that feature is available, you should absolutely use it to track as much data as possible.

There is a WooCommerce Google Analytics Pro plugin, which is currently in development. It does the same thing but uses advanced server-side tracking to send the data to Google Analytics. This can be useful for getting more accurate data. From what was heard of the reports at the time of this writing, this plugin should be released by mid-2015.

Creating an invoice

For some stores, you need to create quotes or invoices for clients instead of being able to give them the typical e-commerce checkout experience. Maybe you need to calculate a custom shipping cost, give the user special pricing, or adjust the order to the quantities you actually have available.

Whatever the reason, you can manually create an invoice for a customer and send it to them. They can then view the invoice and pay for it.

How to do it...

For this recipe, we'll have to manually create a new order, assign the order to your customer, add all of the costs, and then send it to the customer.

1. From the WordPress admin, go to **WooCommerce | Orders**.

2. Click on **Add Order**:

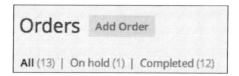

3. Leave **Order status** as **Pending Payment**:

4. Select your customer from the **Customer** dropdown.

It's much easier to already have the customer in your system.
If you have a few extra moments, it's worth adding the customer to your site by going to **Users | Add New** and adding all of their details. When you're adding them, make sure to change their **Role** to **Customer**.

5. Click on the pencil icon next to **Billing Details**.

6. Click on **Load billing address** to load all of your customer details. If you don't have the customer in your system, you can manually fill out their billing details. You must fill out the **Email** field for them to receive any e-mails:

We've set all of the customer details. Now we need to configure the order itself. We'll have to add products, shipping costs, and taxes.

7. Click on **Add line item(s)**:

8. Click on **Add product(s)**.

9. Follow the directions in the pop-up window to add as many products as you like:

10. Once you've added the products to the order, you can adjust the quantities and product price by clicking on the pencil icon to edit the line item:

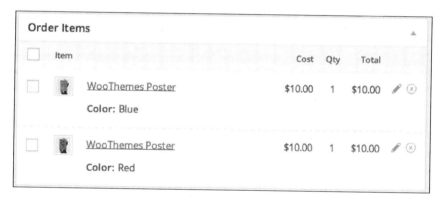

11. Click on **Add shipping cost** and then click on the pencil icon to manually enter the shipping cost and the name of the shipping cost as it appears to your customer (for example, USPS).

12. Once you've added all of the products and shipping costs, click on the **Save** button:

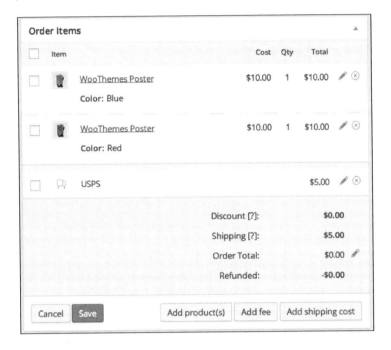

13. Click on **Calculate Taxes**:

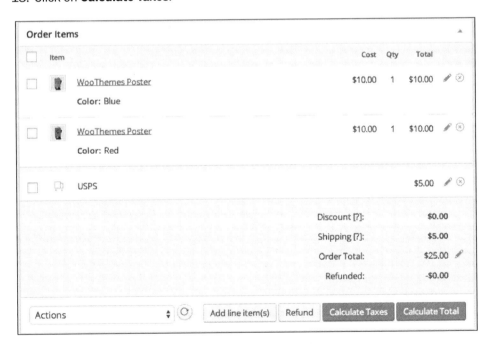

14. Click on **Calculate Total**.

> Alright, we're all done manually creating an order. Now we just need to send it to the customer.

15. Scroll up and click on **Save Order**.

This will send out an e-mail to the customer, letting them know that they have a pending order, with a link to pay for the order. The pending order can also be found on their **My Account** page.

Adding a fee per gateway using the Payment Gateway based Fees extension

Most store owners have preferences when it comes to using certain payment gateways. You might prefer most of your revenue going through a payment gateway that accepts credit cards, like Stripe, but still allow users to use PayPal. For situations like this, you can charge an extra fee on the order based on the payment gateway, to encourage users to use the cheaper option.

Getting ready

You should install and activate the Payment Gateway based Fees extension available on WooThemes.com.

How to do it...

In order to add a fee per gateway using Payment Gateway based Fees, go through the following steps:

1. From the WordPress admin, go to **WooCommerce | Settings | Additional Fees**.

2. Click on the payment gateway that you'll be adding a fee to:

3. Check the **Enable additional fees on total cart value for this gateway** setting.

4. Select how you'd like to charge the additional fee in the **Type of additional fee** dropdown.

Personally, I prefer the **Fixed amount** setting because it's simple for customers to understand.

5. Enter the additional fee in the **Value to add** field.

6. Click on **Save changes**.

During the checkout experience, you'll now see a fee when you select a payment gateway with a fee:

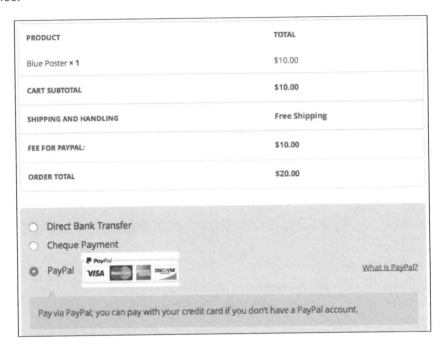

PRODUCT	TOTAL
Blue Poster × 1	$10.00
CART SUBTOTAL	$10.00
SHIPPING AND HANDLING	Free Shipping
FEE FOR PAYPAL:	$10.00
ORDER TOTAL	$20.00

○ Direct Bank Transfer
○ Cheque Payment
◉ PayPal   VISA   MasterCard   DISCOVER   What is PayPal?

Pay via PayPal; you can pay with your credit card if you don't have a PayPal account.

There's more...

In this recipe, I have only covered the options you need to get started. There are a few more options you can tweak to get it working just the way you want. For a full list of options, see the documentation for this plugin at `http://docs.woothemes.com/document/payment-gateway-based-fees/`.

7
Modifying the Checkout Process

In this chapter, we will cover:

- ▸ Adding a Terms & Conditions page
- ▸ Opening the Terms & Conditions page in a pop-up
- ▸ Adding a newsletter signup to the checkout page
- ▸ Adding or removing checkout fields
- ▸ Modifying the image size of related products
- ▸ Adding an Empty Cart button to the cart page
- ▸ Hiding all checkout fields for virtual products
- ▸ Adding banners to remind customers of upgrades
- ▸ Hiding the Coupon field
- ▸ Skipping the cart and going straight to checkout
- ▸ Creating a one-page checkout
- ▸ Adding a default country and state to the checkout page

Introduction

With all of your products in your store, shipping methods set, and payment methods configured, you're all set to accept orders via your store. If you have a bit more energy, you can take your store to the next level and customize your checkout process to make the experience more enjoyable, get more conversions, and increase profits.

For smaller stores that may only offer a few products, you can simplify the experience to get the user through the checkout process as quickly as possible. For larger stores, we can discover related products and upsell the customer in the checkout.

There's a recipe that will let the customer opt in to your newsletter, which is one of the best ways to maintain contact with your customers and remind them to return to your store.

There are plenty of recipes that will minimize the number of steps to purchase your products. If you don't offer coupons, you can hide the coupon fields and prevent your customers from abandoning your store in search of coupons. For stores offering a single product, there is a One Page Checkout plugin that allows you to create an entire e-commerce experience on one page.

At the end of this chapter, you should be able to customize the checkout however you like, depending on your store's needs.

Adding a Terms & Conditions page

It doesn't matter what type of product you sell; there are most likely terms and conditions you would like your customers to be aware of before they check out. These could include your return policy, the software license, or your privacy policy. You could, of course, create a regular WordPress page and add a link in your menu, but that doesn't guarantee that anyone will actually read it.

WooCommerce has a nice feature—a checkbox with a link to the Terms & Conditions page on the checkout page. This forces the user to check that box before completing the transaction. This gives you some assurance that the user actually reads your terms before the purchase and will help you enforce them.

How to do it...

There are two steps to make sure users see your Terms & Conditions page in the checkout. The first stage is to create a regular WordPress page. Perform the following steps:

1. From the WordPress admin, go to **Pages** | **Add New**.
2. Enter a title for the page.
3. Enter the content for the page.

It's pretty common for businesses to use PDFs or Word documents to pass around information. It is easy to upload those documents directly to your site and just link to them, but it's worth the extra time to pull the content out of those documents and paste it right into the Terms & Conditions page. It will make it much easier for your users to read.

4. Click on **Publish**.

Now that we have a page with the terms and conditions, we have to tell WooCommerce which page that is. Let's take a look at the following steps:

1. From the WordPress admin, go to **WooCommerce | Settings | Checkout**.
2. Click on the **Terms and Conditions** drop-down and select your **Terms & Conditions** page.

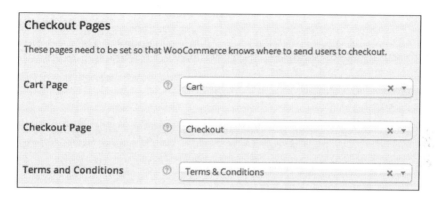

3. Click on **Save changes**.

Now the user will see a checkbox with a link to the **Terms & Conditions** page before the **Place order** button.

There's more...

If you have multiple Terms and Conditions pages, it's best to link to all of them from the main Terms and Conditions page that you set in WooCommerce.

Opening the Terms & Conditions page in a pop-up

One of the secrets to improving your conversion rates is removing everything that isn't essential to the checkout process to keep the user on track. We can improve the checkout experience so that, when the user opens the Terms & Conditions page, it will open in a pop-up. There won't be anything that can distract them, and the only thing they can do is close the window. This should improve your conversion rates.

These distractions were a pain that I felt while using WooCommerce stores, so I built the plugin that we're going to be using in this recipe.

Getting ready

You'll need the WooCommerce Terms and Conditions Popup plugin (available on WooThemes. com) installed and activated on your store. You'll also need to have a Terms & Conditions page set in WooCommerce. See the preceding recipe for more details.

How to do it...

You don't actually have to do anything. This plugin does just one thing and it does it very well. Just by activating the plugin, your Terms & Conditions page will automatically open in a pop-up.

There is one setting we can tweak to make the experience a bit better. By default, the plugin will just load a pop-up that the user can read and then click off to dismiss it. I think it's a better experience to put an **Agree** button at the bottom of the page. Let's take a look at the following steps:

1. From the WordPress admin, go to **WooCommerce | Settings | Checkout**.
2. Check the **Add "Agree" button** setting.

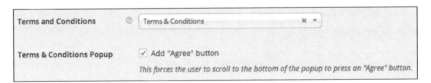

3. Click on **Save changes**.

Now the user will have to scroll down to the bottom of the pop-up and click on the **Agree** button. This will close the pop-up and check the box for the user.

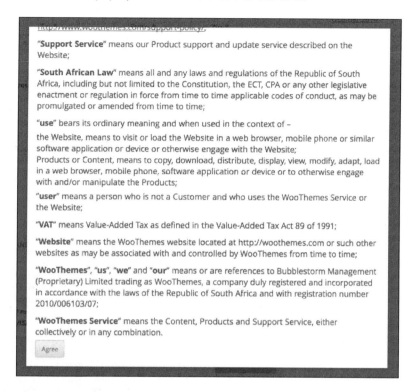

There's more...

Many people have a Terms and Conditions page to protect themselves in case of litigation. If you wish to be thorough and have a record of each customer agreeing to the Terms and Conditions, there is a tutorial by Remi Corson on how to do this at `http://www.remicorson.com/storing-woocommerce-terms-conditions-in-the-database/`.

Adding a newsletter signup to the checkout page

One way to improve how much revenue your store can bring in is to reach out to customers who have already bought something from you. It takes far less energy to get people who have already bought from you to buy a product than it takes to get a new person who hasn't ever heard about you to do the same. Don't forget about your older customers. You should be regularly reaching out to them and letting them know about new products and deals on existing products.

One of the best ways to maintain communication with your existing customers is to let them opt in to your newsletter. You might already have a newsletter signup somewhere on your site, but you might as well offer it to anyone who is going to checkout. Doing so during the checkout process is relatively painless since you're already collecting all of their information. You only need to add a checkbox to the checkout to let the user opt in. The programming will do the rest.

Getting ready

You'll need the Newsletter Subscription plugin (available on WooThemes.com) installed and activated on your site.

You'll also need to either create a **Campaign Monitor** or **MailChimp** account. MailChimp is well known and respected in the web community. They offer a free plan up to 2,000 subscribers, so I recommend setting up a MailChimp account.

How to do it...

In order to add a newsletter signup to the checkout page, take a look at the following steps:

1. From the WordPress admin, go to **WooCommerce | Settings | Newsletter**.

2. Choose your service provider from the drop-down (either **MailChimp** or **Campaign Monitor**).

 You can change the default **Checkbox status** to **Checked**, but I don't recommend it. There isn't much point having a big newsletter list if people aren't interested. As your newsletter list gets bigger (2,000+), you'll have to start paying a monthly fee. It's better to let people opt in and create a highly focused and interested list.

3. Enter your API key in the **API Key** box. You'll need to log in to your MailChimp or Campaign Monitor account and get your API key. The link next to the setting will take you directly to the API page in your account.

API settings

You only need to complete this section if using MailChimp for your newsletter.

MailChimp API Key   [   ]   *You can obtain your API key by logging in to your MailChimp account.*

---

4. Click on **Save changes**.

This will save the page and will also load your newsletter lists in your account. If you don't see any lists, you either haven't created any or you have entered incorrect API information. Let's move on by finally signing up for the newsletter:

5. Once the page refreshes, select your newsletter list.

 If you're using MailChimp, you'll have one extra setting, **Enable Double Opt-in**. This will send an e-mail to the address provided, asking them to confirm they want to join the newsletter. This prevents users from entering a dummy e-mail address and filling up your list. I highly recommend leaving this option on.

6. Click on **Save changes**.

You should now see the ability to opt in to your newsletter on the checkout page.

There's more...

There are dozens, possibly hundreds, of newsletter providers. If you use services such as AWeber, Constant Contact, Mad Mimi, or MailPoet, there are extensions for those services available on WooThemes.com. They have very similar settings pages.

Adding or removing checkout fields

One of the things that WooCommerce excels at is customization. With other platforms, the checkout experience is completely locked down. There's no way you can ask for more information from the customer and no way to remove unnecessary fields. With WooCommerce, we give that power to the store owners and instead prevent them from deleting the essential fields.

As a store owner, you may want to know how people found your site. Did they do a Google search, were they referred by a friend, or did they find you through social media? Those answers could affect how you choose to market your business. Adding a **How did you hear about us?** field to the checkout is pretty painless with the Checkout Field Editor plugin.

Getting ready

You'll need the Checkout Field Editor plugin (available on WooThemes.com) installed and activated on your site.

How to do it...

The Checkout Field Editor plugin gives us additional settings we can tweak to change checkout fields and how they behave. We need to navigate to the right-hand side checkout field area and then add our field. Let's take a look at the following steps:

1. From the WordPress admin, go to **WooCommerce | Checkout Fields**.

    At this point, you'll see the list of billing fields, and a set of tabs along the top of the page. You can choose to put the field under the **Billing** section, the **Shipping** section, or the **Additional Fields** section. For most use cases, I suggest putting the additional fields in the **Additional Fields** section. That way, if there's another plugin that modifies the billing or shipping fields, your custom field should be unaffected.

2. Click on **Additional Fields**.

3. Click on **+ Add field**.

4. Enter a name for the field. The name is only used in the code and won't be displayed to the end user. I'll name my field `hear_about_us`.

5. Now select the type of field you want to add. In our case, we want to give the user a list of options and we're going to choose the **Select** type.

> If you want to give a user a set of options, it's best to use either the **Select**, **Multiselect**, or **Radio** option. The **Radio** option works well enough, but needs a bit of fiddling to make it look like it fits into the checkout experience. If you don't mind tinkering with CSS, use radio buttons. If you don't want to touch the CSS, the **Select** or **Multiselect** option is your best bet. The **Select** field is a drop-down that allows the user to select one option. The **Multiselect** field is the same thing but allows them to select multiple options.

6. Now enter a label for the field. This is visible to the user. We'll enter `How did you hear about us?`.

7. Now we need to enter the possible values a user can select. Put those values in the **Placeholder / Option Values** field. Each value should be separated by a pipe character (|).

> With the **Select** box, it's a good idea to start the list of values with an extra pipe character. This will create a blank option so the **Default** dropdown option will be blank. Otherwise, the **Default** option will be the first value and users might just skip the field.

8. To make the field look as good as possible, I recommend setting the **Position** setting to **Full-width**.

9. You can optionally make the field **Required** by selecting that option from the **Validation Rules** field.

10. Click on **Save Changes**.

Your saved field settings should look something like this:

And, on the frontend, your field should look something like this, depending on your theme:

There's more...

You can, of course, also use this plugin to remove or edit existing fields. The plugin will prevent you from editing anything critical, but it's always a good idea to test your checkout after any changes to make sure that it still works smoothly.

You can use more than just radio buttons and select boxes. You can also add text boxes, text areas, checkboxes, password fields, and date pickers.

Modifying the image size of related products

Built right into WooCommerce is the ability to **cross-sell** and **upsell** products. By cross-selling and upselling your products, you can very easily increase your average order value.

Cross-sells are products that work well together (such as peanut butter and jelly). Cross-sells appear on the cart page to get the customer to buy more products. Upsells are similar products where you want the customer to buy the more expensive option, for example, a generic version of peanut butter upselling a well-known and popular brand of peanut butter. These appear on the Product page.

The one adjustment I'd made to the WooCommerce cross-sell is to make it a bit bigger. If you're going to cross-sell something, you should make sure it's big enough to catch the customer's eye on the cart page.

Getting ready

You'll need to have at least two products in your store.

How to do it...

The first step is to configure one product to cross-sell the other product. Once the product is set up, we can customize the cart page. Let's take a look at the following steps:

1. In the WordPress admin, click on **Products** and navigate to one of your products.
2. Scroll down to the **Product Data** panel.
3. Click on **Linked Products**.
4. Enter the product you wish to cross-sell in the **Cross-Sells** field.

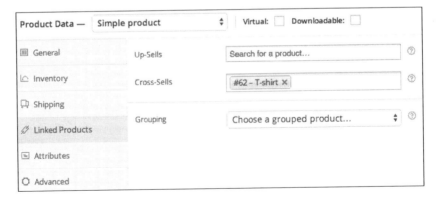

5. Click on **Update**.

   Now that the cross-sell is set, we can take a look at how it's displayed on the frontend of the site.

6. Go to the frontend of your site.

7. Add the product to your cart.

8. Go to the cart page.

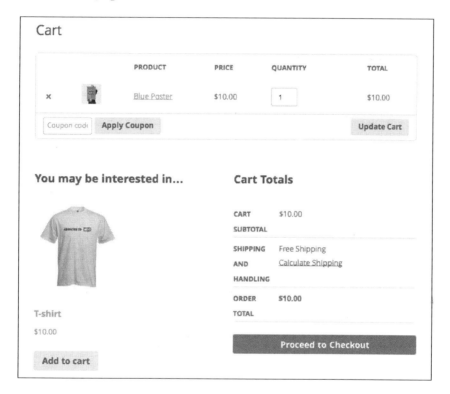

The cross-sell is definitely visible. There's enough space for two cross-sells, but you may prefer to have a really big image and try harder to sell one product.

To make this more visible, we'll have to do three different things via code: increase the size of the product image, add some CSS to display the image in as large a way as possible, and force the page to only display one cross-sell. Add the following code to the bottom of your theme's `functions.php` file or create a custom plugin:

1. First, we need to increase the size of the product image. We have to remove the existing programming (that's the `remove_action` line) and then add our own custom programming (that's the `add_action` line). The `add_action` line at the very bottom gets the whole thing running. Carry out the following code:

    ```php
    function woocommerce_cookbook_big_upsell_image() {
        if ( class_exists( 'WooCommerce' ) && function_exists(
    'woocommerce_get_product_thumbnail' ) ) {
            if ( is_cart() ) {
                remove_action(
    'woocommerce_before_shop_loop_item_title',
    'woocommerce_template_loop_product_thumbnail', 10 );
                add_action(
    'woocommerce_before_shop_loop_item_title',
    'woocommerce_cookbook_product_thumbnail', 10 );
            }
        }
    }

    // get a bigger version of the product thumbnail.
    function woocommerce_cookbook_product_thumbnail() {
        echo woocommerce_get_product_thumbnail( 'large' );
        echo woocommerce_cookbook_product_thumbnail_css();
    }
    add_action( 'woocommerce_before_shop_loop_item_title',
    'woocommerce_cookbook_big_upsell_image', 0 );
    ```

2. Below the preceding code shown here, paste in the following. This code will make sure that the item is displayed at its full width:

    ```php
    function woocommerce_cookbook_product_thumbnail_css() {
        echo '<style>
            .woocommerce .cart-collaterals .cross-sells
    ul.products li, .woocommerce-page .cart-collaterals .cross-
    sells ul.products li{
                width: 100%;
            }
        </style>';
    }
    ```

3. Lastly, we need to make sure that we only display one cross-sell on the page. Two big cross-sells would look bad. Add the following code beneath the rest:

```
add_filter( 'woocommerce_cross_sells_total',
'woocommerce_cookbook_cross_sells_total', 10 );
function woocommerce_cookbook_cross_sells_total( $total ) {
    return 1;
}
```

4. Save and upload your file.

You should now see just one big cross-sell image on the cart page.

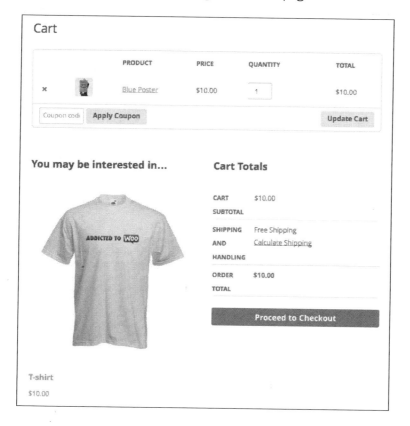

 If you're not seeing any cross-sells, make sure they aren't already in your cart.

There's more...

For the sake of simplicity, in this tutorial I wrote the CSS inline. This isn't necessarily a best practice. If you wanted to make this code a bit prettier, you could take that CSS, put it in a style sheet, and enqueue the style sheet with `wp_enqueue_style`.

Rather than having to manually set which products are related to each other, there's a service called **Graphflow** that does this for you. They use an algorithm to constantly revaluate which products you should recommend to which customers. They have a free tier and a WooCommerce plugin. Find out more about the service and a link to their plugin at `http://graphflow.com/`.

Adding an Empty Cart button to the cart page

If you have the type of store where people are constantly comparing prices, adding products to their cart, removing them, and then starting all over again, it might be worth your while to add in an **Empty Cart** button.

WooThemes keeps WooCommerce as light as possible. An empty cart button is useful to some stores but it takes up valuable space in other stores. For that reason, it isn't included in WooCommerce. As with many other enhancements, there is a free plugin that can do this for us.

How to do it...

Adding the empty cart button is really simple. To get started, we need to add a plugin. Work through the following steps:

1. In the WordPress admin, click on the **Plugins** menu and click on **Add New**.
2. Look for the **Woocommerce Empty Cart Button** plugin.
3. Install and activate the plugin.

And this is all we have to do. This plugin does just one thing and does it well. There aren't any settings. The plugin adds the **Empty Cart** button and that's it.

How it works...

This plugin adds some extra HTML to the list of products on the cart page. The plugin also contains a function that listens for a button push and then empties the cart.

There's more...

If you want to style the **Empty Cart** button, it already has a class assigned to it. You can use the `emptycart` class.

Hiding all checkout fields for virtual products

WooCommerce is pretty smart. If you only have virtual products such as memberships or downloadable products in the cart, WooCommerce won't ask for any shipping information. But some people want to take this a step further. They don't want all of the billing details—they only want the bare minimum information.

WooCommerce doesn't automatically remove these fields because some payment gateways require more billing information. If your payment gateway doesn't require billing details, then you could do this and make the checkout process a bit smoother. The best way to find out if your payment gateway allows this is to try the following code snippet and do a test purchase.

How to do it...

We'll have to add some code to our `functions.php` file in our theme or create a custom WooCommerce plugin.

1. At the bottom of your theme's functions.php file, add the following code to change the checkout fields that are displayed to the user:

```
// Remove unnecessary checkout fields
add_filter( 'woocommerce_checkout_fields' ,
'woocommerce_cookbook_remove_checkout_fields' );
```

2. The code here calls a function, but we haven't written it yet. We now need to write the function that alters the checkout fields. Add the following to the bottom of the file:

```
// remove unnecessary checkout fields function
function woocommerce_cookbook_remove_checkout_fields(
$fields ) {
    // check if the cart needs shipping
    if ( false == WC()->cart->needs_shipping() ) {
        // hide the billing fields
```

```
        unset($fields['billing']['billing_company']);
        unset($fields['billing']['billing_address_1']);
        unset($fields['billing']['billing_address_2']);
        unset($fields['billing']['billing_city']);
        unset($fields['billing']['billing_postcode']);
        unset($fields['billing']['billing_country']);
        unset($fields['billing']['billing_state']);
        unset($fields['billing']['billing_phone']);
        // hide the additional information section

        add_filter( 'woocommerce_enable_order_notes_field',
    '__return_false' );
    }

    return $fields;
}
```

3. Save the file and upload it to your site.

Now, when the cart contains exclusively virtual products, you should only see the name and e-mail fields.

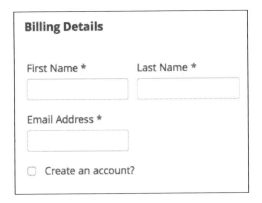

How it works...

This code only does one thing—it checks to see if the cart requires shipping and then it unsets the unnecessary fields. You could remove some of those unset lines to keep some fields (for example, the phone field) if you need them.

There's more...

A word of caution about removing checkout fields: the more information you can give the payment gateway, the easier it is for them to determine if purchases are legitimate. You could have an increase in fraud if you don't ask for billing details such as country, state, postcode, and so on. If you do have an increase in fraud, start adding the fields back in or use a payment gateway such as Pay With Amazon, which uses billing information that's already been verified on their end.

Adding banners to remind customers of upgrades

There are a number of rewards and discounts that you could offer to your customers. Maybe you unlock free shipping at $100 or you give the customer a 5% discount at $200. Unless you use a lot of screen real estate to promote these rewards, most customers won't know about them or act on them. One way around this would be to list the different rewards and how close the customer is to reaching them. If you have good rewards, people will buy more products to reach the reward. This can drastically increase your average order value.

Getting ready

Set up free shipping so that it's unlockable at $100. This is covered in *Chapter 5, Setting Up Shipping Methods*. You will also need to install and activate the Cart Notices plugin, available on WooThemes.com.

How to do it...

In order to add a banner to remind your customers of upgrades, refer to the following steps:

1. Go to **WooCommerce | Cart Notices**.

   From here, we can see all of the cart notices on the site. We can also see a list of short codes we could use to display the cart notices on other pages on the site.

2. Click on **New Notice**.

3. Select the **Type of notice** you want to create. We want to create a **Minimum Amount** notice.

 If you want to know how each notice works, you can select the type and some helper text will appear beneath the field, describing how it works.

4. Enter a name for the notice. This is only for your reference, so put whatever makes sense. Since we're creating a notice about free shipping, I'm going to call mine Free Shipping.

5. Make sure the **Enabled** checkbox is checked.

 If you want to pause a promotion or create one in advance, uncheck the **Enabled** checkbox.

6. Enter the message you want to display to customers in the **Notice Message** setting. The default message is perfect for our use case.

7. If you have a page describing the free shipping reward, you can add a button that links to the page by filling in the **Call to Action** and **Call to Action URL** fields.

8. Enter $100 in the **Minimum Order Amount** field.

9. Click on **Create Cart Notice** to save your settings.

If you add a product to your cart, it will look something like the following on the cart page:

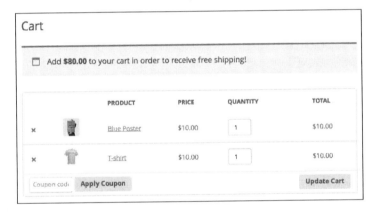

And if you hit the minimum order amount, the message disappears.

There's more...

This plugin is very powerful. You can also recommend that users buy certain items in bundles, or let them know that, if they order on the weekend their packages won't ship until Monday; alternatively, if a certain product is in the cart, you can have them read your review of a related product. You can create as many notices as you like.

Hiding the Coupon field

There are several studies that show that having a coupon field in your checkout process can actually lower conversion rates. When people see a coupon field, they assume they can find a coupon somewhere online and they'll leave your site looking for a coupon. It's better to hide the field and give your special customers a discount another way.

Using URL Coupons, we can share special URLs like `http://mysite.com/holiday2015` to give people a special discount. These URLs could be shared on your newsletter, via social media, on business cards, or even mentioned on podcasts.

Getting ready

You will also need to install and activate the URL Coupons plugin, available on WooThemes.com.

How to do it...

We'll be creating a WooCommerce coupon, configuring a few extra settings, and then hiding the coupon field on the cart and checkout pages. Let's take a look at the following steps:

1. Go to **WooCommerce | Coupons**.
2. Click on **Add Coupon**.
3. Name the coupon. For normal coupons, customers have to type in the name, so you want to avoid spaces or weird characters. With URL coupons, you don't need to worry about that—feel free to name it anything you like.
4. Set the **Discount type** and **Coupon amount** fields as you would any other coupon.

5. In the **Unique URL** field, add the URL you wish to add on to your main site. If you have a holiday special, then you might want to enter `holiday2015`. The full URL that someone would have to type in would be `http://mysite.com/holiday2015`. Let's take a look at the following screenshot that illustrates the usual coupon settings page with a few extra settings provided by the URL Coupons extension:

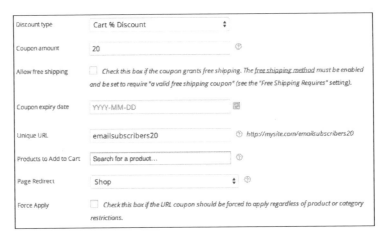

 If you want to have a promotional page that describes the promotion the user just unlocked, then you should first create a WordPress page and enter the URL for that page. If you just want to direct the user to your shop, then you'll have to set the **Page Redirect** setting.

6. Click on **Publish**.

When the user visits the page, they'll see a banner saying the coupon code was applied successfully and they'll see the coupon details on the cart page.

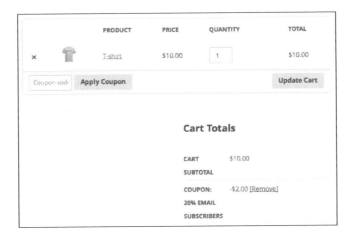

Now that we have set up the URL coupons, we can disable the regular **Coupon** field. Implement the following steps:

1. From the WordPress admin, go to **WooCommerce | Settings | Checkout**.
2. You'll notice that there are a few new settings on this page related to coupons. Enable both **Hide on cart page** and **Hide on checkout** page.
3. Click on **Save changes**.

There's more...

You can do a lot with this plugin. If you have coupons that apply to certain products, you can configure the coupon to automatically add those products to the cart and then redirect the user to the cart. It makes the whole experience very quick and easy for the user.

Skipping the cart and going straight to checkout

This recipe will be useful for you if you have the type of store where most people only buy one product and thus the cart isn't very useful. In such cases, you might want to remove the cart altogether and have the customer skip the cart page and go straight to the checkout.

 We have covered a similar recipe, *Making the Add to Cart button go straight to the checkout page*, in *Chapter 3, Changing the Product Organization*, which uses a plugin instead of code.

Getting ready

In the WordPress admin, you need to make sure the **Redirect to the cart page after successsful addition** option under **WooCommerce | Settings | Products | Display** is checked.

How to do it...

We'll be writing a bit of code to change the page that a customer lands on after adding a product to the cart. You'll want to put this in either your theme's `functions.php` file or in a custom plugin. Let's take a look at the following steps:

1. Open either your theme's `functions.php` file or a custom plugin file.

2. At the bottom of the file, add the following code:

```
// make the add to cart redirect go to the checkout page
function woocommerce_cookbook_add_to_cart_redirect() {
    return get_permalink( wc_get_page_id( 'checkout' ) );
}
add_filter( 'woocommerce_add_to_cart_redirect',
'woocommerce_cookbook_add_to_cart_redirect' );
```

3. Save the file and upload it to your site.

How it works...

This code doesn't replace the cart page entirely. It just skips the cart page when a product is added to the cart. A user can still access the cart if it's in your menu or if they type in the direct URL. This could be ideal, because some people will want to return to their cart after leaving the site.

There's more...

We used the `wc_get_page_id( 'checkout' )` line to select the checkout page. You could use that same function to get the link to any WooCommerce page and the user would be directed to that page. To see the other WooCommerce pages you can access with that function, view the documentation for that function at `http://docs.woothemes.com/wc-apidocs/function-wc_get_page_id.html`.

Creating a one-page checkout

WooCommerce was designed as a full-fledged e-commerce platform. Even if you use all of the features, there may be times where you want to have a special promotion and you don't need the full cart. For these times, there is the WooCommerce One Page Checkout extension, which can turn any page into a checkout page for a product or set of products. This is the perfect landing page for those store owners who use their newsletters to send out promotions; it's also good for people who want to have a custom checkout for some of their products.

Getting ready

You can create a one-page checkout with one product, but this recipe will show you how to do it with two or more products. You should have two products for this recipe.

You'll need the WooCommerce One Page Checkout plugin (available on WooThemes.com) installed and activated on your site.

How to do it...

We don't actually need to change any checkout settings. The default checkout will work just fine. We actually do everything through regular WordPress pages and **shortcodes**. Let's take a look at the following steps:

1. From the WordPress admin, go to **Pages | Add New**.

2. Enter a title for the page in the **Title** field.

3. In the space where you would normally type in page content, note the new button that looks like a shopping cart.

4. A pop-up will appear and you can start typing the names of your products in the **Products** field. An autocomplete field will help you select the exact product.

5. Select **Product Table** as **Template**.

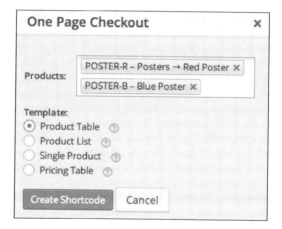

There are four different templates at the time of this writing, and all of them have their uses. **Single Product** is obviously good if you only offer one thing on this page. **Pricing Table** is great when you have very similar products with features you can list in a table. **Product List** is great for similar products that don't need pictures and where the user can only select one option. **Product Table** is great for products that are different and where the user may want several different products.

6. Click on **Create Shortcode** and you'll notice that some text (called a shortcode) is automatically inserted in the content of the page.

7. Feel free to add anything you like before or after that shortcode.

8. Click on **Publish**.

On the frontend of your site, you should see a one-page checkout similar to this:

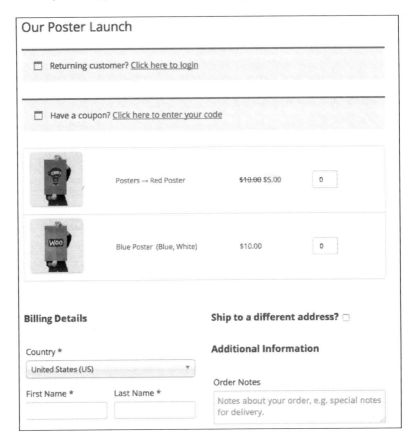

How it works...

The text you see on the page after clicking on **Create Shortcode** is what controls the programming. If you ever want to edit how the one-page checkout works, it would be best to go through the process of creating the shortcode again. A typo in the shortcode could break the programming, so be careful. Click on the shopping cart icon button, go through the steps, and create a new shortcode. Then delete your old one.

There's more...

The WooCommerce One Page Checkout plugin integrates very nicely with the Easy Pricing Tables plugin mentioned in *Chapter 4, Running a Membership Site*.

Adding a default country and state to the checkout page

If you are just starting out, you may not have a very wide reach, you may not have any international orders, and you might not even have orders from outside your state or province. If that's the case, why make people type it in? With a touch of code, we can set some defaults that will help people get through the checkout process.

How to do it...

This code can either go in your theme's `functions.php` file or in a custom WooCommerce plugin. Let's take a look at the following steps:

1. Open either your theme's functions.php file or a custom plugin file.

2. We'll start by setting just the default country. At the bottom of the file, add the following code:

```
add_filter( 'default_checkout_country',
'woocommerce_cookbook_default_checkout_country' );
// change the default country to USA function
woocommerce_cookbook_default_checkout_country() {
    return 'US';
}
```

3. If you also want to set a default state, you'll have to add a bit more code. In the following code sample, I'll set the default state to Colorado:

```
add_filter( 'default_checkout_state',
'woocommerce_cookbook_default_checkout_state' );
// change the default state to Colorado
function woocommerce_cookbook_default_checkout_state() {
    return 'CO';
}
```

 If you want to change the default country to something other than the US, you'll have to find out the country's two-letter code. A Google search will uncover this. If you want to change the default state to something other than Colorado, you'll have to replace the two-letter state code of Colorado, CO, to your state code.

4. Save the file and upload it to your site.

Make sure you're logged out of your site, add a product to your cart, and proceed to check out. You should see the state and country filled in by default.

8
Managing Orders and Taxes

In this chapter, we will cover:

- Sending a note to a customer
- Refunding an order
- Importing orders from another store
- Sending order information to third parties with the Advanced Notifications plugin
- Making the order numbers sequential
- Giving away products
- Manually entering tax rates
- Automatically calculating tax rates with the TaxJar plugin
- Setting a post code for correct taxation with the Local Pickup setting

Introduction

Running an e-commerce store still involves quite a bit of work to manage the store and fulfill your orders. You'll have to know how to communicate with customers, how to refund orders, and how to give away sample products. The first set of recipes in this chapter tells you how to perform all of those essential functions.

WooCommerce is very flexible and there are plugins to help you customize your order numbers to match an existing system, to send order notifications to third parties for drop-shipping, and to import orders from an existing store.

The last set of recipes in this chapter is all about taxes. There are recipes to help you set up taxes yourself and there is also a recipe that shows you how to integrate with a third-party service that will handle all of the taxes for you.

Sending a note to a customer

You may occasionally need to reach out to customers and let them know something about their order. Maybe the order is delayed or maybe you want to ask them if you could swap one product for an equivalent product. When that happens, you'll want it all documented in one place. You don't want to use e-mail to do this because, a year down the line, you won't know why you did what you did. That's why WooCommerce has the built-in ability to contact a customer from the order page; the outgoing message is logged on that page.

Getting ready

You'll need an order in your store. If you don't have an order yet in your store, make a test order using the Bank Transfer gateway.

How to do it...

Communicating with customers can be done directly from the order page, by performing the following steps:

1. From the WordPress admin, go to **WooCommerce | Orders**.

2. Click on any of the orders.

3. On this page, you'll see the **Order Notes panel** and, at the bottom of the panel, there will be a field called **Add note**.

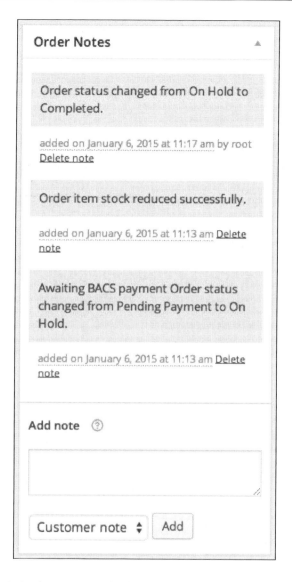

4. Enter your note to the customer in the **Add note** field.

 Customer notes can contain HTML. So, if you want to embolden or italicize something in your message, you could type in the HTML manually.

5. Click on **Add**.

As soon as you click on **Add**, the e-mail will be sent out. This e-mail uses the WooCommerce e-mail template. WooCommerce templates can be customized; refer to the *Overriding WooCommerce templates* recipe in *Chapter 9, WooCommerce Theming*, to see how to do this.

A note has been added to your order

Hello, a note has just been added to your order:

Just letting you know your order will be **one day late** due to the holiday.

For your reference, your order details are shown below.

Order #143

Product	Quantity	Price
T-shirt	1	$10.00

There's more...

The Order Notes section also allows you to leave private notes. These are great for when a customer calls or messages you via social media or some other medium and you want to record the conversation. You can do this by changing the select box under **Add note** to **Private note**.

 Only the outgoing message is recorded in the **Order Notes** section. If you need to log a customer's response, you should use the **Private note** setting.

Refunding an order

No matter how good your product is, at some point you'll have to refund an order. In just about any e-commerce system, you can manually log in to your payment gateway such as PayPal or Stripe and reverse the charges. That works, but it's tedious and, if you have anyone helping you, you'll have to give them access to your payment gateway, which not every store owner will feel comfortable with.

WooCommerce can do refunds directly from the order screen. This is a huge time saver because you don't have to go into the payment gateway. It also reduces errors because you're clicking on the **Refund** button from within the order itself instead of refunding a charge in the payment gateway, which you would have to cross-reference.

Getting ready

Most payment gateways support refunds directly on the order page. Both PayPal and Simplify Commerce support these refunds. So do Stripe and many other popular gateways.

You'll need an order in your store—preferably one created using a gateway that supports refunds on the order page. I'll be refunding a payment made through Stripe.

How to do it...

An order can be refunded from the order page in WooCommerce by performing the following steps:

1. From the WordPress admin, go to **WooCommerce | Orders**.
2. Click on one of your orders that was processed by a gateway that supports refunds.

3. If you scroll down the **Order Items** panel, you'll see a list of items, at the bottom of which is a **Refund** button.

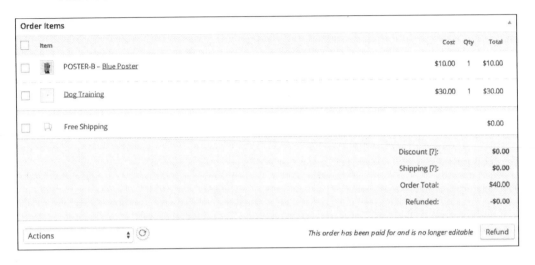

4. Once you click on the **Refund** button, a new panel will slide open.

5. You can enter the full amount or a partial amount in the **Refund amount** field.

6. You can optionally fill in the **Reason for refund** field. This is logged along with the refund for your own information and won't be shared with the customer.

7. Click on the button that does not say **Refund manually**. My button says **Refund $40.00 via Stripe**.

8. A pop-up window will confirm the refund. Click on **Ok**.

A loading icon will appear for a moment while all of the data is refreshed on the page. Then you're done.

 If you only see a button that says **Refund manually**, then your gateway doesn't support refunds or it isn't configured correctly.

Importing orders from another store

It's really convenient to have a list of all of your orders in one place. If you have previously used another system for e-commerce, you don't want to have to log in to multiple accounts to see whether someone made a purchase at one time. You also want all of your analytics in one place. It would be a shame to not see the growth of your store in one graph. You want to have all of that data in one place so you can get the most out of reports.

For these reasons, WooThemes released an importer to help users import their orders, customers, and even coupons.

Getting ready

You'll need the Customer/Order/Coupon CSV Import Suite plugin, available on WooThemes. com, installed and activated on your site.

You'll also need a CSV file to import. A sample CSV file you can import will be covered in this recipe.

How to do it...

The first part of the recipe is making sure your CSV is in the right format. The easiest way to copy the right format is to download the sample file and then use that as a base.

1. From the WordPress admin, go to **WooCommerce | CSV Customer Import Suite**.
2. Click on **Sample Order CSV** and it will be downloaded.
3. Open the downloaded file in a program such as Microsoft Excel, Numbers on Mac, or Calc in Google docs (this can be accessed for free via your web browser).

Once you've opened up the file you'll see a giant list of fields. Along the top will be the field labels. And the others rows will have some dummy data in them. All of the dummy orders in this are formatted correctly, so if your CSV file looks similar to this, then it should import correctly:

	A	B	C	D	E	F	G	H	I	J	K
1	order_nu	order_nu	date	status	order_sh	order_sh	tax_item	tax_item	cart_disc	order_dis	order_tot
2	WT-817	817	5/1/14	complete	0	0	label: Lo	label: Sta	0	0	15.99
3			5/1/14	complete	0	0	0		0	0	15.99
4	WT-1021	1021	5/3/14	processing			label: Sta	0	0	0	36.47
5	WT-1022	1022	5/4/14	pending	0	0	0	0	0	0	66.6

You can either delete the dummy order data and manually type in your orders or, if you have a ton of orders and that's too much work, you can use your existing CSV and then rename the headers along the top so they match the headers in the dummy CSV.

Formatting the CSV can take some time and, if you name a column incorrectly, it could create problems down the line. If you have problems importing some data, it's most likely because a column was incorrectly labeled or the value in the column isn't in the right format.

Once you have the CSV file in the right format, you can import it by performing the following steps:

1. From the WordPress admin, go to **WooCommerce | CSV Customer Import Suite**.
2. Click on **Import Orders**.
3. Fill in the **Choose a file from your computer** field.

> You could use the **OR enter path to file** field, but that involves uploading a file via FTP and there could be permission issues. It's far easier to use the regular file picker. The Delimiter field is there in case your CSV file, for some reason, uses a different character to separate the fields. A CSV file is so named because all of the values should be separated by a comma (Comma Separated Values), but some systems do use a semicolon or other separators for separating values. You should be able to choose a delimiter when you save or export a CSV file when using an application such as Microsoft Excel, Mac Numbers, or Google Docs. When in doubt, just leave the delimiter as a comma.

4. Click on **Upload file and import**. You'll be taken to an advanced settings screen.

I highly recommend checking the **Dry Run** setting so that, if you do format something incorrectly, you don't have to spend much time fixing the mistake.

5. If you're trying to import the sample file, you'll most likely have to check the **Allow Unknown Products** setting.

6. Click on **Submit**.

The upload will start. It may take a while if you have hundreds or thousands of orders. When you're done, you'll see a report that will tell you whether there were any problems:

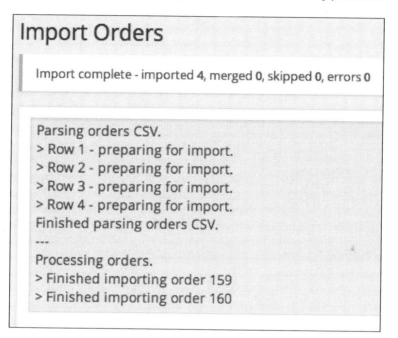

Import Orders

Import complete - imported 4, merged 0, skipped 0, errors 0

Parsing orders CSV.
> Row 1 - preparing for import.
> Row 2 - preparing for import.
> Row 3 - preparing for import.
> Row 4 - preparing for import.
Finished parsing orders CSV.

Processing orders.
> Finished importing order 159
> Finished importing order 160

If you find any problems, you can delete the successful orders in the CSV, double-check whether the incorrect orders are in the right format, and then retry the upload.

When you're done, you should be able to see the orders by clicking on **WooCommerce** in the main menu of the WordPress admin.

There's more...

If you want to export a CSV file from one WooCommerce store and import it into another store, you can use the Order / Customer CSV Exporter plugin, also available on WooThemes.com.

Sending order information to third parties with the Advanced Notifications plugin

If you have to work with manufacturers or drop-shippers, then you have to have some way to let them know that you've received an order and they should start producing or sending products. This doesn't have to be limited to drop-shipping—it could also be a partner, an employee who just ships the products, or some other usage. With the Advanced Notifications plugin, you can send notifications to anyone, based on which products were in the cart.

You can also send notifications for all sorts of activity in your store, such as products being low on stock, out of stock, or when backorders are made. For this example, we'll be sending a **drop shipper** an e-mail when an order gets placed.

Getting ready

You'll need the Advanced Notifications plugin, available at WooThemes.com, installed and activated on your site.

You'll also need a product already created on your site.

How to do it...

To send out notifications, we need to create a recipient in the notification settings and then set a recipient on the edit product page, by performing the following steps:

1. From the WordPress admin, go to **WooCommerce | Notifications**.
2. Click on **Add notification**.
3. Fill in the **Recipient name** and **Recipient email address(s)** fields.
4. Leave the **Plain text** field unchecked.
5. Select **Purchased** from the **Enable notifications** field.
6. Leave **Notification triggers** blank.

If you have a lot of products that send notifications, then you could create a category and send the notification for any products in that category. You can configure this with the **Notification** field. If you are sending a notification for one or two products, it's best to do this on the product page, which we'll do now.

7. Optionally, check the **Include prices** and **Include order totals** fields, depending on how much information the recipient needs.
8. Click on **Save changes**.

Now that we have a recipient, we can send them a notification on a per product basis. We will set this on the product page in the WordPress admin by performing the following steps:

1. In the WordPress admin, click on **Products** and then navigate to any product.

2. On the **Product data** panel, you'll see a **Notifications** text box.

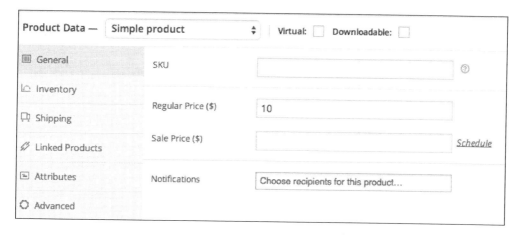

3. Click on the box and select your recipient(s).

4. Click on **Update**.

There's more...

A more sophisticated way to configure these notifications is to create a shipping class for all of your drop-shippers. Then you can set a notification for the drop-shipper based on the shipping class of the product. This can be done through the **Notification triggers** field.

Making the order numbers sequential

WordPress uses the same ID system for pages, posts, media, products, and orders. That means that, if you add a new product and an image for that product, the next order will be three numbers higher than the previous order. As a store owner, employee, or anyone not familiar with the inner workings of WordPress, that might be confusing.

In the e-commerce world, with accounting software, drop-shippers, customers, and everything else going on, it's really helpful to have consecutive order numbers. There is a free plugin that will make all order numbers sequential.

How to do it...

We can install the WooCommerce Sequential Order Numbers plugin by performing the following steps:

1. In the WordPress admin, click on the **Plugins** menu and then on **Add New**.

2. Run a search for the `WooCommerce Sequential Order Numbers` plugin.

3. Install and activate the plugin.

There isn't any configuration necessary for this plugin. By simply installing it, all future order numbers will be in the correct order.

There's more...

There is a lot more you can do with order numbers. You may want to set a prefix or, suffix, or choose the starting order number, for example, `Pat_0001`. This can be done with a premium version of the same plugin called **Sequential Order Numbers Pro**, which is available on WooThemes.com.

Giving away products

If you often have customers switch one product for another or if you have a downloadable product that you want to give away to customers, then it can be a bit of a pain to manually create an order. You could manually type in their information, run a search for the products, set the payment and shipping info, and then save the order. That does work, but it's time-consuming.

To speed things up, there's a handy extension that asks you for a customer name, asks you for one or more products you're giving away, and then creates the order for you. It probably cuts the amount of time you spend giving away a product in half.

Getting ready

You'll need the WooCommerce Give Products plugin, available at WooThemes.com, installed and activated on your site.

How to do it...

Giving away products with this extension can be done on the special Give Products page by filling in a few fields and clicking on a button:

1. From the WordPress admin, go to **Products | Give Products**.

2. Type in the customer's name, e-mail, or ID into the customer field and click on the correct autosuggestion.

3. Type in the product you wish to give the user and click on the correct autosuggestion. You can enter as many products as you wish to give away.

Give Products

Select a user by typing their display name, email address or user ID here:

root (#1 – @woothemes.com) ▾

Select products by typing in their names, variation details or IDs here (you can select as many products as you like):

Blue Poster – #42 (SKU: POSTER-B) ✕

Give product(s)

4. Click on **Give product(s)**.

The extension will do all the hard work of creating the order for you and sending the customer an email, letting them know they were gifted a product. If it's a downloadable product, they'll also receive a link to the product.

Manually entering tax rates

E-commerce isn't all fun and games, of course. You do have obligations to operate lawfully and to pay taxes. WooCommerce doesn't know the tax rates unless you connect it to a third-party service or enter them manually.

In the United States, it's typical that you have to pay state tax when the buyer is in a state where you have your nexus. **Nexus** means a physical presence such as an office or warehouse.

You can enter your tax rates manually into WooCommerce. Once the user enters their location during the checkout process, WooCommerce will automatically calculate the taxes and add them to the total.

Getting ready

You'll have to consult a tax expert to determine the tax rates you need to enter into your store. You could have federal rates, state rates, municipality rates, zip code rates, and more. It all depends on the laws of your business and the laws of the buyer.

How to do it...

Using the following steps, we first set our basic tax settings and then enter our rates:

1. From the WordPress admin, go to **WooCommerce | Settings | Tax**.

2. Make sure the **Enable taxes and tax calculations** setting is enabled. Otherwise, WooCommerce will skip right over the tax calculations.

3. Choose if you want to enter your prices with or without taxes by choosing an option for the **Prices Entered With Tax** field. In the US, it's common to enter prices without taxes.

4. Choose whether you want to display prices with tax included or with tax excluded by choosing an option for the **Display Prices in the shop** select box. In the US, it's common to display prices without taxes.

5. Choose an option from the **Calculate Tax Based On** drop-down. If you are operating in the US, you may want to select **Customer billing address**. Please consult with a tax expert to verify whether this is the best option for your store.

6. Click on **Save changes**.

   We've configured our basic settings. Now we need to enter our rates.

7. Go to the **WooCommerce | Settings | Tax** page and click on **Standard Rates**.

   On this page, we can enter as many rates as we need.

8. Click on **Insert row**.

9. Enter the **Country Code, State Code, ZIP/Postcode, City**, or whatever is appropriate to determine your tax rate.

> For a tax that applies to the entire state of Colorado, I would enter the **Country Code** and **State Code**. If I had a tax rate that applies to a specific city in Colorado, then I would enter the **Country Code, State Code**, and **City**. You don't need to enter more information than necessary.

10. Enter the tax rate in the **Rate %** column.

11. Add a name for the tax in the **Tax Name** field. This could be as simple as `Colorado state tax`. Please check with your accountant whether the tax needs to be called by a specific name.

12. Enter a number for the **Priority** field. The priority is used to limit one tax rate per priority. So, if there is no reason someone should be billed taxes for two different zip code ranges, make sure they have the same priority and only the first matching rate will apply. If you want to have a national tax rate, a state tax rate, and a city tax rate, make sure they're all using different priorities. You could have one priority for all national rates, another for state rates, and yet another for all city rates.

13. You can optionally check the **Compound** and **Shipping** settings. Your tax expert can let you know how the taxes should be applied and if you need to apply them to shipping costs or whether the tax rate needs to be compounded.

14. Click on **Save changes**.

How it works...

On the checkout page, as soon as the customer enters their address, WooCommerce will calculate the applicable taxes, add them to the total, and display it to the customer, as shown in the following screenshot:

PRODUCT	TOTAL
Blue Poster × 1	$10.00
CART SUBTOTAL	$10.00
COLORADO STATE TAX	$0.50
ORDER TOTAL	$10.50

There's more...

If you don't want to consult with a tax expert, there are several tools you can use to calculate the tax rates for you. Refer to the next recipe to learn more about a third-party service that does it all automatically.

You can also see the official documentation at `http://docs.woothemes.com/document/setting-up-taxes-in-woocommerce/`.

Automatically calculating tax rates with the TaxJar plugin

If you already know a tax expert or you already know the tax rates, then it isn't too much of a pain to enter the tax rates manually. But if you don't know a tax expert, then it's a bit of work and it's probably cheaper and faster to use a third-party tool to calculate the tax rates for you.

One such tool that's geared for US businesses is **TaxJar**.

Getting ready

You should sign up for a TaxJar account. They have a 30-day free trial.

How to do it...

Using the following steps, we first download the free TaxJar plugin from WordPress.org:

1. In the WordPress admin, click on the **Plugins** menu and then on **Add New**.
2. Run a search for the `TaxJar - Sales Tax Automation for WooCommerce` plugin.
3. Install and activate the plugin.

   Now that we have the plugin installed, we have to configure it.

4. From the WordPress admin, go to **WooCommerce | Settings | Integrations**.
5. If TaxJar is the only integration you've installed, it will automatically be loaded. Otherwise, click on **TaxJar**.
6. Make sure the **Enable TaxJar** setting is checked.
7. Enter your API token in the **API Token** field. If you don't know where to find that in TaxJar, click on the link underneath the field.
8. Enter the **Ship From Zip Code** and **Ship From City** fields.
9. Click on **Save changes**.

Your store will contact TaxJar to calculate taxes before displaying them to the customer at checkout.

 If you have multiple addresses, you can enter these in TaxJar and they'll make sure to check against these extra addresses while checking tax rates.

There's more...

At the start of 2015, Europe introduced new legislation for taxing downloadable goods (such as e-books, video courses, and so on) being sold in the European Union. This affects all sellers and not just sellers in Europe. If you are selling digital goods to Europe, you should look into **VATMOSS**. One popular service that checks and calculates these rates for you is **Taxamo**.

For more information, go to `http://www.woothemes.com/2014/12/handling-eu-vat-woocommerce/`.

Setting a post code for correct taxation with the Local Pickup setting

If you're selling to people in different parts of the country or the world, you normally base the tax on the location of the customer. For that reason, you don't normally have to set your own zip code or city. But if you sell to people outside your city most of the time, but also have the Local Pickup shipping method selected, then you'll need to set your zip code and city.

How to do it...

This is an edge case, so there isn't any way to do this in the admin. You have to do this with some custom code, using the following steps:

1. Open your theme's functions.php file, located under `wp-content/themes/your-theme-name/`, or create a custom WooCommerce plugin.

2. At the bottom of the file, enter the following lines of code to set your city:

```
add_filter( 'woocommerce_countries_base_city' ,
'woocommerce_cookbook_countries_base_city' );
function 'woocommerce_cookbook_countries_base_city'() {
    // Replace with your store town/city
    return 'Townland';
}
```

3. In this snippet, replace `Townland` with the name of your city.

4. And, below that, add the following lines of code to set your zipcode:

```
add_filter( 'woocommerce_countries_base_postcode' ,
'woocommerce_cookbook_countries_base_postcode' );
function woocommerce_cookbook_countries_base_postcode() {
    // Replace with your store postcode / zipcode
    return '45040';
}
```

5. Replace 45040 with your actual zip code.

Now that you've set your city and zip code, the Local Pickup method will use those for taxation. You still need to set the rates. See the *Manually entering tax rates* recipe we've covered earlier.

WooCommerce Theming

In this chapter, we will cover:

- ▶ Declaring support for WooCommerce
- ▶ Displaying the accepted credit cards
- ▶ Adding a cart icon to the menu
- ▶ Overriding WooCommerce templates
- ▶ Using WooCommerce hooks
- ▶ Displaying an image on the category archive page
- ▶ Writing CSS to customize the Add to Cart button
- ▶ Creating a product slideshow
- ▶ Removing a product category from the Shop page

Introduction

With hosted e-commerce platforms, you're limited to customizing the areas they let you customize. With a platform such as WooCommerce, which is open source, you can customize just about anything. Many themes have user-friendly controls for the most common customizations and, for the things that you can't change via the admin area, you can change with code. Even if you can't change something with code, there are many developers out there willing to do it.

There are many modifications you can make with plugins that are freely available, for example, displaying the credit cards you accept and adding a cart icon to the menu. And there are plenty of things you can change with code. You can override any of the WooCommerce templates, use the hooks built into WooCommerce to add extra programming, and do plenty of other things.

This chapter will focus on the code in rather more detail. Many users want to make their store reflect their brand and they like to customize every little detail. That's why this chapter will emphasize the code—so that you can customize every detail as you like.

If you haven't yet picked a theme for your e-commerce store, a great starting point is the Storefront theme from WooThemes. It's available for free on WordPress.org; go to `https://wordpress.org/themes/storefront/`.

Declaring support for WooCommerce

If you're developing a theme from scratch or if you're using a theme that wasn't designed to work with WooCommerce, you may see a notice on your site when you install WooCommerce. The following screenshot displays the theme-incompatibility message:

This message can be easily dismissed by clicking on **Hide this notice** but, if you're planning on distributing this theme to others, then it's nice to let people know you designed your theme to work with WooCommerce.

Getting ready

You'll need to install a theme that shows the notice shown in the preceding screenshot. If your theme doesn't show this notice, then it's already declared support for WooCommerce and you can skip this recipe.

If you're a theme developer, you may have heard of Underscores. This starter theme hasn't declared support for WooCommerce, so if you base your theme on Underscores, you'll need to declare support. See the Underscores website for more information at `http://underscores.me/`.

How to do it...

Declaring that your theme supports WooCommerce takes a pretty small code snippet. We'll add that code snippet to your theme's `functions.php` file and then we'll be done. In the following steps, we declare support for our WooCommerce theme:

1. Open up your theme's `functions.php` file in your code editor.

2. Add the following code to the bottom of your `functions.php` file:

```
add_action( 'after_setup_theme',
'woocommerce_coobook_support' );
function woocommerce_coobook_support() {
    add_theme_support( 'woocommerce' );
}
```

3. Save and upload the file.

How it works...

It's worth noting that adding this code only hides the notice. It doesn't automatically make your theme work with WooCommerce. You should go through all of the WooCommerce pages and make sure that everything looks correct.

Displaying the accepted credit cards

Every credit card has a different transaction fee. Many credit cards charge around 2 percent, but some cards such as American Express can charge 4 or 5 percent. For this reason, some retailers only accept certain cards through their payment gateway. If you don't allow one of those cards, it's best to tell the customer that ahead of time.

If you support every credit card, you still can show the customer a list of supported cards. They'll be more likely to convert knowing that you support their credit card.

How to do it...

There is a plugin that does exactly this. It allows you to select exactly which cards you support. In the following steps, we install this plugin and display the list of cards accepted for payment purposes:

1. In the WordPress admin, click on the **Plugins** menu and then on **Add New**.
2. Run a search for the `WooCommerce Accepted Payment Methods` plugin.
3. Install and activate the plugin.

    Now that we have installed the plugin, we need to configure the settings.

4. Go to **WooCommerce | Settings | Checkout**.
5. Scroll down to the **Accepted Payment Methods** section.

6. Check all of the credit cards that apply.

Accepted Payment Methods

To display the selected payment methods you can use the built in widget, the `[woocommerce_accepted_payment_methods]` shortcode or the `<?php wc_accepted_payment_methods(); ?>` template tag.

American Express	☐ Display the American Express logo
Bitcoin	☐ Display the Bitcoin logo
Cash on Delivery	☐ Display Cash on Delivery symbol
Dankort	☐ Display the Dankort logo
Discover	☐ Display the Discover logo
Google	☐ Display the Google logo
Maestro	☐ Display the Maestro logo
MasterCard	☑ Display the MasterCard logo
PayPal	☑ Display the PayPal logo
Visa	☑ Display the Visa logo

---

7. Click on **Save changes**.

   We've determined which credit cards we accept. Now we need to display that on the frontend. We'll be doing this by using a widget that comes bundled with the WooCommerce Accepted Payment Methods plugin.

8. From the WordPress admin, go to **Appearance | Widgets**.

9. Click on **WooCommerce Accepted Payments** from the **Available Widgets** area and select the widget area where you would like to place it.

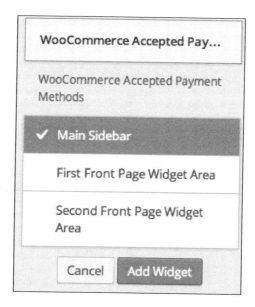

10. Click on **Add Widget**.

11. If you like, you can change the title of the widget.

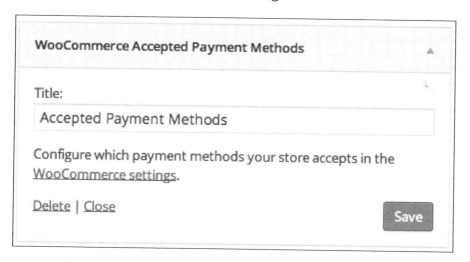

12. Click on **Save**.

If you visit the frontend of your site, you should see the list of accepted payment methods.

ACCEPTED PAYMENT METHODS

PayPal VISA

There's more...

Displaying the list of accepted payment methods in a widget is just one way to display them. You could also use a shortcode to display them on a page or a template tag to place it anywhere in your theme. You can find out the exact syntax by reading the WooCommerce Accepted Payment Methods plugin's documentation on WordPress.org.

Adding a cart icon to the menu

Users like to be able to view both the number of items and the total value that they have in their cart. If you can display this information on every page, then users won't have to constantly check the cart page. They should have to spend less time double-checking their numbers and get through your site quicker. This should improve your conversion rates.

Getting ready

Before we begin, you should have a menu already created in WordPress. We'll be adding the cart icon to that menu.

How to do it...

The following steps demonstrate a plugin that allows you to add a cart icon to the menu and provides several options that you can customize:

1. In the WordPress admin, click on the **Plugins** menu and then on **Add New**.
2. Run a search for the `WooCommerce Menu Cart` plugin.
3. Install and activate the plugin.

   This plugin works for WooCommerce and other WordPress e-commerce platforms. That's great, but it does mean that the settings are a bit harder to find.

4. Go to **Settings | Menu Cart Setup**.

5. Leave the **Select which e-commerce plugin you would like Menu Cart to work with** setting set to **WooCommerce**.

6. Enter the menu you wish to add this cart to in the **Select the menu(s) in which you want to display the Menu Cart** field.

7. You can optionally display the cart when it's empty by checking the **Always display cart, even if it's empty** field.

> I'm not a fan of letting users make mistakes. Unless you have some sort of marketing promotion on the cart page or something else for users to do on that page, I recommend hiding the cart until they add something to it.

8. Enable the cart icon by checking the **Display shopping cart icon** field.

9. You can optionally change the alignment of the cart by choosing one of the options for the **Select the alignment that looks best with your menu** setting.

> To make the cart icon easier to find, I recommend changing the alignment. So if your menu is aligned left, then align the cart icon to the right. It will stand out for the user, which will make it easier to understand.

10. Click on **Save Changes**.

If you go to the frontend of your site and add a product to your cart, you should see the new cart icon in the menu.

WooCommerce
Just another WordPress site

| HOME | CART | CHECKOUT | MY ACCOUNT | **SHOP** | 🛒 1 ITEM - $10.00 |

There's more...

If you want to make the cart icon even more noticeable, you can use CSS to style that menu item. You can apply CSS to the `wpmenucartli` class.

There is a pro version of this plugin available (as if you didn't see all of the annoying promotions in the settings page). I haven't personally felt the need for it, but there are more options if you need them.

Overriding WooCommerce templates

If you've ever wanted to change the layout of the single product page, the cart page, or even one of the e-mails sent out by WooCommerce, you can do that by overriding the templates in WooCommerce. If you're familiar with WordPress theme templates, they are very similar. If you copy a WooCommerce template to your theme, WooCommerce will load your template instead of the default template that is in the plugin.

Being able to overload any template in WooCommerce means you can customize every aspect of how WooCommerce looks to your customers. If you want to remove something, change something, or add something new, that's all possible.

For our purposes, we'll be adding some CSS classes to the HTML. If we can reuse existing CSS classes that we've already styled, then that saves us a lot of time as we won't need to rewrite those styles.

Getting ready

You need to have at least one product in your store.

How to do it...

Overriding WooCommerce templates is similar to using a child theme and overriding templates in the parent theme. The first step is to copy an existing file in the WooCommerce plugin to your theme. You can copy any file in the `templates` folder in WooCommerce to a `woocommerce` folder in your theme.

For example, you could copy `woocommerce/templates/single-product.php` to your-`theme/woocommerce/single-product.php`. In the following steps, we discuss in more detail overriding the WooCommerce templates:

1. Using your regular file browser, navigate to the `WooCommerce` plugin folder and copy `templates/single-products/tabs/tabs.php` to `woocommerce/single-products/tabs/tabs.php` within your theme.

2. Using your code editor, open up the `tabs.php` file we just copied to your theme.

3. Look for this line of code: `<div class="woocommerce-tabs">`.

   This div element wraps around the tabs. We're going to add a CSS class to that line to help style it.

4. Add a blank space and append this line of code right after `woocommerce-tabs`:

   `tabs-wrapper`

5. Save and upload the file.

How it works...

WooCommerce will run a search for any templates that you may have overridden and use those instead of the file that comes with the WooCommerce plugin. You could override one template or every single template if you wanted.

There's more...

You can do just about anything to these files. We added a CSS class that will help with styling, but you could just as easily add or remove extra HTML, JavaScript, or PHP.

When you update to a new version of WooCommerce, make sure your templates still work. It's rare, but sometimes templates need to be updated and, if you have out-of-date templates, something could break. You can check the status of your templates in the WordPress admin, under **WooCommerce | System Status**.

If you ever have out-of-date templates, copy the new files from the updated WooCommerce plugin to your theme and then modify the new files to include your old changes.

Using WooCommerce hooks

The ability to override WooCommerce templates is available to alter HTML and CSS. It isn't terribly great when adding extra logic with PHP or rearranging different templates. Many of the templates are *hooked* in. What this means is that there is a placeholder in the template that will usually look similar to the following code:

```
/**
 * woocommerce_single_product_summary hook
 *
 * @hooked woocommerce_template_single_title - 5
 * @hooked woocommerce_template_single_rating - 10
 * @hooked woocommerce_template_single_price - 10
 * @hooked woocommerce_template_single_excerpt - 20
 * @hooked woocommerce_template_single_add_to_cart - 30
 * @hooked woocommerce_template_single_meta - 40
 * @hooked woocommerce_template_single_sharing - 50
 */
do_action( 'woocommerce_single_product_summary' );
```

From the comments in the code, you can see where the developers have programmed certain pieces of functionality. However, they're not easy to move unless you know how to use WordPress hooks.

The regular product page looks as shown in the following screenshot:

For our example, we'll be moving the product rating lower down the product page, after the product SKU and category.

Getting ready

You need at least one product with a review in your store.

How to do it...

This recipe only has two lines of code, but both of those lines have a lot of parameters in them. Follow the recipe to see how the hooks work. At the end of the recipe, there will be a link to provide more explanation on each line of the code.

There are only two things you can do with hooks: add something to them or remove something from them. Using the following steps, we'll start by removing one of the actions from a hook:

1. Open up your theme's functions.php file or a custom WooCommerce plugin.

2. At the bottom of the file, add the following code:

```
remove_action( 'woocommerce_single_product_summary',
'woocommerce_template_single_rating', 10 );
```

This code removes a specific action on a certain hook at a certain priority. If you get one of the preceding three parameters wrong, it won't work.

Now that we've removed the review, we want to add it back in after the category and SKU information.

3. Below the last line of code, add the following:

```
add_action( 'woocommerce_single_product_summary',
'woocommerce_template_single_rating', 45 );
```

4. Save and upload the file.

The rating is now below the **Category** and **SKU**, as illustrated in the following screenshot:

How it works...

The hooks in WooCommerce use the hooks system built into WordPress. You can learn all about hooks on Wordpress.org at `http://codex.wordpress.org/Plugin_API/Hooks`.

There's more...

There are hundreds of hooks in WooCommerce and all those hooks allow you to modify the way WooCommerce works. The best place to look for hooks is within the code itself.

Displaying an image on the category archive page

Each category page in WooCommerce looks the same, with of course the exception of the products in that category. This works great for a lot of merchants. However, some merchants like to differentiate their categories—maybe add a banner at the top of the category page to help users see at a glance what they're looking at, or some other customization.

By building on our knowledge of hooks from the preceding recipe, we can add an action onto an existing hook and display a category image.

Getting ready

You need at least one product and it needs to belong to a category. You should also have an image to represent that category.

How to do it...

In the following steps, we're going to start off with something really easy. WooCommerce allows you to upload an image for a category, but it doesn't display it anywhere by default. Once we get the image uploaded, then we can add some code to display it:

1. From the WordPress admin, go to **Products | Categories**. You should see a list of categories as shown in the following screenshot:

Image	Name	Description	Slug	Count
	fruit		fruit	0
	Posters		posters	2

2. Hover over any category and click on **Edit**.
3. Click on **Upload/Add Image**.
4. Then select a photo from your media library or add a new photo.
5. Click on **Update**.

    We've added an image to a category. Now we need to write a function that will display that category image.

6. In your code editor, open up your theme's `functions.php` file or a custom WooCommerce plugin.

7. Add the following code to the bottom of the file:

```
function woocommerce_cookbook_category_image() {
    if ( is_product_category() ){
        global $wp_query;
        $cat = $wp_query->get_queried_object();
        $thumbnail_id = intval( get_woocommerce_term_meta(
$cat->term_id, 'thumbnail_id', true ) );
        $image = wp_get_attachment_url( $thumbnail_id );
        if ( $image ) {
            echo '<img src="' . esc_url( $image ) . '"
alt="" />';
        }
    }
}
```

We have a function to display the image, but we haven't told the function when to run. We need to add one more line to do this.

8. Below the code we just added, add one more line:

```
add_action( 'woocommerce_archive_description',
'woocommerce_cookbook_category_image', 2 );
```

9. Save and upload the file.

You should now see the image on the category page, as shown in the following screenshot:

How it works...

This code uses the same hooks system that was discussed in the preceding recipe. The function is hooked in at the right time by using an action. The function checks to make sure we're on a category page, then it looks in the database for an image that's associated with the category. If it finds one, it prints the image to the page.

Writing CSS to customize the Add to Cart button

You can do quite a bit with customizing templates and using hooks, but neither of those actually focuses on how things look. If you want to change the way something looks, such as the size, color, text family, border color, and so on, then you'll have to use **Cascading Style Sheets** (**CSS**) to do that.

WooCommerce already has basic styles for everything included in the plugin, so you don't have to write anything. But if you want to change something, then you'll have to write some styles to override the default styles.

Getting ready

You should have a simple product in your store.

How to do it...

If you take a look at a simple product on the frontend of your store, the **Add to Cart** button that comes with it looks pretty simple, as shown in the following screenshot:

There are actually dozens of styles applied to the button, some of which are applied to all buttons and some just to the button on the product page. In the following steps, we're going to start by writing some styles that affect all WooCommerce buttons:

1. In your code editor, open your theme's `style.css` file.

2. At the bottom of the file, add the following code:

```
woocommerce button.button, .woocommerce input.button {
    font-size: 1.2em;
}
```

This code will increase the font size of all WooCommerce buttons. WooCommerce buttons are styled in such a way that, as the font inside the box grows, the box itself will grow. Therefore, you just need to increase the font size and the button will grow. Now we want to style just the button on the product page.

3. Add the following code beneath the code we saw earlier:

```
.woocommerce button.single_add_to_cart_button {
    text-shadow: 1px 1px 1px #333;
}
```

4. Save and upload the file.

You'll be able to see the larger button with a text shadow on the single product page, as shown in the following screenshot:

How it works...

CSS is one of my favorite tools. It's basically a pattern-matching system. If the elements on the page match the pattern, then the styles get applied to that HTML element. You can write really specific styles that apply to only one element on one page or something that gets applied to every page.

In this case, we're using one of the most useful properties of CSS—overriding styles. You don't need to override everything, just the one or two styles you want to change. You can change the background color of the button without affecting anything else, which is really powerful.

There's more...

This is just the tip of the iceberg when it comes to writing and styling WooCommerce. If you want to write more CSS, then I recommend the free tutorials at `http://www.w3schools.com/`.

If you plan on customizing every aspect of the styles, then you could also remove the default stylesheet and write yours from scratch. Look into the `wp_dequeue_style` function, which is documented at `http://codex.wordpress.org/Function_Reference/wp_dequeue_style`.

Creating a product slideshow

Slideshows are a great way to highlight different products in your store. Some themes have slideshows built-in, but then you're very limited in terms of how you would like to configure them. You might only be able to place a slideshow on the home page or you might only be able to include so many slides. Built-in slideshow themes are pretty limiting and it's not considered a good practice to look for this sort of functionality in a theme. Instead, if you can find a slideshow in a plugin, those are usually a bit more flexible in terms of placement and exactly how you want the slides to work. We'll be using the WooSlider and WooSlider – WooCommerce Products Slideshow plugins together to create a slideshow of products that link to the specific product pages.

Getting ready

You'll need the WooSlider and WooSlider – WooCommerce Product Slideshow plugins, available at WooThemes.com, installed and activated on your site.

How to do it...

The beauty of using a plugin is that we can place this slideshow on any page we want. In the following steps, I'll be placing this slideshow on the sample page that's created when you install WordPress. You can choose to put it on any page, including the home page.

1. In the WordPress admin, click on **Pages**.
2. Find the page where you wish to place the slideshow.
3. Click on the title of that page to edit it.
4. Click on **Add Media**. A modal window will pop up.
5. Click on **Slideshows**.

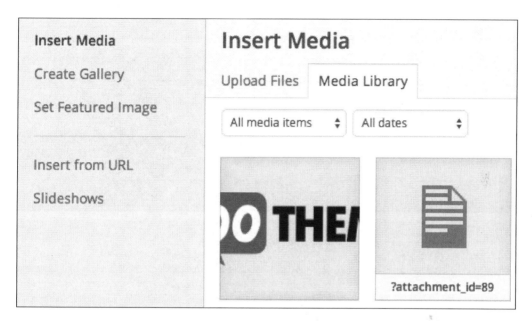

6. Select **Products** as the **Slideshow Type**.
7. Select how many slides you want through the **Number of Products** setting.
8. You can optionally add an Add to Cart button right on the slide with the **Display "Add to Cart" button** setting.

 I don't think you need to clutter up the slideshow with a button. Users will likely want to know more about the product before they purchase anything, so they'll probably click on the product title to get more information and there's already an **Add to Cart** button on that page.

9. You can now select what products appear in the slideshow by choosing a category, a tag, featured products only, or sale products only. You can select any mix of these that you like with the **Categories**, **Tags**, **Featured products only**, and **On sale products only** settings.
10. I recommend letting users click through to the product pages by enabling the **Link the Slide Title to the product** setting.

11. Click on **Insert Slideshow** and you'll see a shortcode has been created and inserted into the content of the page.

12. Click on **Update** to save the page.

If you view the page on the frontend, you'll see your slideshow as shown in the following screenshot:

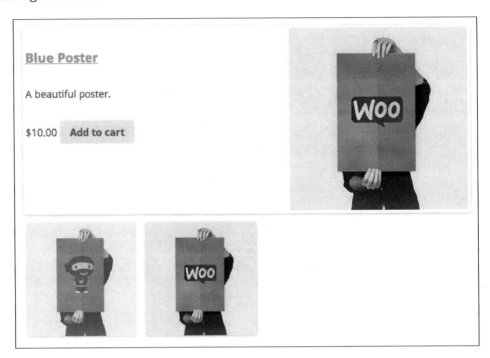

There's more...

In addition to showing off products, WooSlider can slide anything. You could very easily create some promotional images that show multiple products in each image, link to the appropriate category.

Removing a product category from the Shop page

You may have some products that you don't want to advertise to the entirety of your audience. Maybe they're products that only apply to one gender, or products that are only good for someone of a certain age, or some other niche product that doesn't make sense for your whole audience. If you make sure that the products appearing on the shop page apply to everyone, that will keep your conversion rates high.

How to do it...

To remove a product category from the Shop page, we'll have to modify the query to the database. We can use some of the hooks built into WordPress to modify the query rather than writing an entirely new one, which is a huge time-saver. Let's perform the following steps to remove a product category:

1. In your code editor, open up your theme's `functions.php` file or a custom WooCommerce plugin.

2. At the bottom of the file, add the following code:

```
add_action( 'pre_get_posts',
'woocommerce_cookbook_pre_get_posts_query' );
function woocommerce_cookbook_pre_get_posts_query( $q ) {
    if ( ! $q->is_main_query() ) return;
    if ( ! $q->is_post_type_archive() ) return;
    if ( ! is_admin() && is_shop() ) {
        $q->set( 'tax_query', array(array(
            'taxonomy' => 'product_cat',
            'field' => 'slug',
            'terms' => array( 'posters' ),
            'operator' => 'NOT IN'
        )));
    }
    remove_action( 'pre_get_posts',
'woocommerce_cookbook_pre_get_posts_query' );
}
```

3. You'll need to change the posters in the code to the slug of the category you wish to exclude. If you want to exclude multiple categories, you should comma-separate them and make sure that each one is enclosed in single quotation marks. For example, `'category-1', 'cat-2', 'cat3'`.

 If you don't know the slug of the category you wish to exclude, you can see the full list in the WordPress admin under **Products | Categories**.

4. Upload and save the file.

How it works...

This code is run right before WordPress queries the database. The first part checks to make sure we're modifying the right query you wouldn't want to accidentally break your blog page. Once we know we're only modifying the right query, we tell WordPress to ignore certain product categories. And that's it. It takes a bit of code to do what we want to do, but it's pretty simple.

There's more...

You could modify all types of queries and all sorts of things with queries. You could, for example, have a shop page that only shows featured products that were released in the last month. But queries of this type are very advanced and you'll probably need a developer to help you with that sort of thing.

10
Exploring More with WooCommerce

In this chapter, we will cover:

- ▶ Enabling WooCommerce Reviews
- ▶ Hiding reviews from the Category/Shop Page
- ▶ Displaying positive reviews in the product description
- ▶ Cloaking an affiliate link
- ▶ Creating a regular expression for a cloaked affiliate link
- ▶ Creating a coupon with restrictions
- ▶ Bulk-generating coupons with the Smart Coupons plugin
- ▶ Changing the default e-mail's from address
- ▶ Sending follow-up e-mails after purchase

Introduction

We've covered everything you need to get your store up-and-running—the fun parts, such as configuring your products, and the less fun parts, such as configuring taxes and managing orders. There are, however, a few recipes that didn't fit cleanly into other chapters but I still thought important to share.

Product reviews are a big step in the buying process. Knowing that someone else tried it and they're either satisfied or not satisfied helps customers in making their decision. We have several ways to highlight reviews or make the reviews less prominent if you have a few reviews that aren't flattering.

We haven't talked about affiliate marketing and how you can market others' products on your store. We'll talk about ways to make affiliate links more user-friendly and a way to create groups of affiliate links.

We'll also cover ways to generate coupons in huge batches, how to send customers follow-up e-mails, and a few extra things on top of all that.

Enabling WooCommerce Reviews

It's one thing to write good things about your product, and it's entirely different if someone else writes good things about your product. One of the best ways to get users to trust your brand is to enable reviews. Positive reviews can reinforce your own claims. Negative reviews can also be useful by showing the limits of your products. Some people will want to see that information, and you can capture that by displaying product reviews.

How to do it...

Enabling reviews on your site is very similar to enabling WordPress comments. Let's take a look at the following steps:

1. From the WordPress admin, go to **WooCommerce | Settings**.
2. Click on **Products**.
3. Scroll down to **Reviews** and you'll see several options.

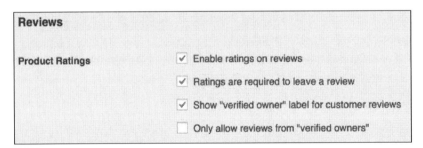

4. Make sure the **Enable ratings on reviews** setting is checked.

> I recommend enabling both **Ratings are required to leave a review** and **Show "verified owner" label for customer reviews**. The first will make sure people leave a legitimate review. If you don't force a user to say why they're leaving a one-star review, you can't do much about it. The second setting is good for showing users that the reviewer is a legitimate owner. There's less chance the review could be fake.

5. Click on **Save changes**.

There's more...

To make sure your customers can definitely leave a review, you should log out of your site, go to the product page, and make sure there's a form that lets you leave a review. If it isn't there, then there could be something wrong with your theme.

There is a recipe in this chapter that will show you how to automatically send follow-up e-mails to customers. This is an excellent way to get reviews on your site.

Hiding reviews from the Category/Shop page

You may like the idea of reviews but also have a few angry customers who are lowering the average rating of your product. You don't want that to impact future customers. One solution is to hide the average rating on the shop page and only show ratings on the product page, where users will be able to read the content of the review in addition to the actual star rating. That will help them understand exactly why someone doesn't like the product and the reason may not even affect them, so you could still get the sale.

How to do it...

If you look at the shop page right now, it will display a star rating based on an average of all of the reviews, as shown in following screenshot:

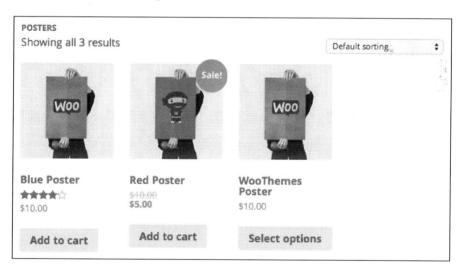

The star rating is added to the page with an action attached to a hook. We're going to use the hook system to remove that action. Let's take a look at the following steps:

1. Open up your theme's `functions.php` file or a custom WooCommerce plugin.

2. Add the following code to the bottom of the file:

```
remove_action( 'woocommerce_after_shop_loop_item_title',
'woocommerce_template_loop_rating', 5 );
```

3. Save and upload the file.

There's more...

There are tons of hooks in WooCommerce that you can take advantage of. You can add or remove actions that will change when a specified programming action takes place or if it takes place at all. If you want to have an idea of what can be moved around, look at the templates located in the `woocommerce` plugin under `templates`.

There is a tutorial in the *Using WooCommerce hooks* recipe in *Chapter 9, WooCommerce Theming*, that shows you how to take advantage of these hooks.

Displaying positive reviews in the product description

If you do have brand evangelists praising your products, you should make sure their reviews are visible. If you have products that are hard to justify, some social affirmation that other people enjoy the product will be a huge benefit. If that's the case, you might want to highlight a product review in the product description to make sure every user sees it.

Getting ready

You need to have a product with at least one review in your store.

How to do it...

There aren't any plugins that do this. We'll have to custom-code this by ourselves. Unlike many of the code snippets I've shared, this one is a bit lengthier and is broken up into several pieces. Let's take a look at the following steps:

1. Open up your theme's `functions.php` file or a custom WooCommerce plugin.

2. The first step is to tell WordPress to run a custom function at a specific point on the product page. At the bottom of the file, add the following code:

```
add_action( 'woocommerce_single_product_summary',
'woocommerce_cookbook_single_review', 25 );
```

3. Now we actually need to write that function. Add the following code right beneath the preceding lines of code:

```
function woocommerce_cookbook_single_review() {
    // get all of the comments
    $args = array ('post_type' => 'product');
    $comments = get_comments( $args );
    // get the best comment
    $best_comment = woocommerce_cookbook_get_best_comment(
$comments);
    // if there is a best comment then print it
    if ( $best_comment > 0 ) {
        woocommerce_cookbook_print_best_comment(
$comments[$best_comment] );
    }
}
```

This code gets all of the comments for a product and then sends them to a function that picks the best comment. If this function gets a best comment, it sends the comment to a different function that prints it. If you ran this code right now, it would break the page. We still need to write those two extra functions. In our case, these two functions will be woocommerce_cookbook_get_best_comment and woocommerce_cookbook_print_best_comment.

4. Add the following code to the file:

```
function woocommerce_cookbook_get_best_comment( $comments )
{
    $best_comment = 0;
    // loop through each comment to find the best
    foreach( $comments as $key => $comment ) {
        // get the rating
        $rating = intval( get_comment_meta( $comment-
>comment_ID, 'rating', true ) );
        // save the rating in the comment
        $comment->rating = $rating;
        // if the rating is higher, it's approved, and
there are at least 10 characters, save it
        if ( $rating > 0 &&
$rating > $comments[$best_comment]->rating &&
'1' == $comment->comment_approved &&
10 < strlen( $comment->comment_content ) ) ) {
            // save the array key of the comment
            $best_comment = $key;
        }
    }
    return $best_comment;
}
```

This function looks for the best comment. It will go through the entire list of comments and look for the highest-rated review that is approved and has at least 10 characters. It then returns the index of that comment to the original function.

If we get a best comment, we now need to write one last function to display it.

5. Add the following code to the file:

```
function woocommerce_cookbook_print_best_comment ( $comment
) {
    // print out the best comment and some very basic
styles
    ?>
    <p>Here's what people are saying about this
product:</p>
    <blockquote class='comment-text'>
        <?php echo apply_filters( 'comment_text', $comment-
>comment_content ); ?>
    </blockquote>
    <style>
        .comment-text{
            font-style: italic;
        }
    </style>
    <?php
}
```

This function prints out any comment that gets passed in as well as some very basic styles to visually separate it from other content.

6. Save and upload the file.

If you take a look at the frontend of your site, you should see the review in the product description.

There's more...

There are many ways to take this even further. You could change the code to show two comments, you could change the display on the frontend to make it stand out even more, or you could make the experience nicer by linking the comment in the top to the comments in the bottom. When you write custom code, you can do just about anything.

Cloaking an affiliate link

One of the topics we haven't really touched on is **affiliate marketing**. You don't have to sell just your products. You can use WooCommerce to create product pages for other people's products as well and link them to a site where you have an affiliate deal. You could be recommending related products or you could have an entire store that's nothing but affiliate products.

To track affiliate traffic, the site owner will usually give you a special link that you have to use. Sometimes, they look pretty normal; for example, `http://mywebsite.com/?ref=25`.

And some other times, they look pretty scary; for example, `http://shareasale.com/?ref errer=4234242342&target=243534534543&otherboringdata=23424234234`.

When the links don't look pretty, some users may get scared off. So you can set up a special URL on your site that points to the affiliate URL. On your site, you'll use the pretty link, and that will take the user to the affiliate URL. This is called **link cloaking**.

How to do it...

For this example, I'll be creating a link on my site that will take the user to an affiliate URL. Let's take a look at the following steps:

1. In the WordPress admin, click on the **Plugins** menu and then on **Add New**.
2. Run a search for the **Redirection** plugin.
3. Install and activate the plugin.

    The Redirection plugin is a very useful plugin for changing any links on your site. If you have links that point to a page that no longer exists, you can create a redirect to take the user to a more useful page. You can use this same functionality for affiliate links.

4. From the WordPress admin, go to **Tools | Redirection**.

5. You should see a list of redirections (it should be empty) as well as a place to enter new ones:

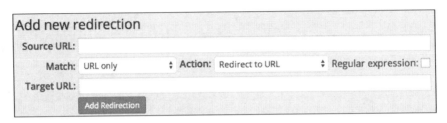

6. Enter the pretty URL that you want your customers to see in the **Source URL** field.

> Rather than typing in `http://mysite.com/affiliate-name/`, you may just type in `/affiliate-name/`.

7. Enter the ugly affiliate URL in the **Target URL** field.

8. You can leave the other fields as they are.

9. Click on **Add Redirection**.

10. Test your link to make sure it works.

There's more...

This is only the very beginning of link cloaking and affiliate marketing. In the next recipe, we'll use regular expressions to create a pretty affiliate link pattern.

Creating a regular expression for a cloaked affiliate link

No one wants to do things hundreds of times. If there's a way you can automate something, you should. This applies when you're uploading thousands of products as well as when you have a ton of affiliate links. If you recommend multiple affiliate links on one site, you can use a pattern-matching technology called **regular expressions** to create affiliate links on-the-fly. This way, you don't have to create a cloaked link for every single product.

It also makes it very easy to manage affiliate links. Sometimes, affiliate links change due to a change on the vendor's side. When that happens, if you use a regular expression, you only have to change the link in one place. If you have hundreds of affiliate links, you'll have to change each one manually.

Getting ready

You need to have the Redirection plugin installed and know how to create a basic cloaked link. See the preceding recipe, *Cloaking an affiliate link*, to know more about this.

How to do it...

The first thing we need to do is find a pattern in the URL structure of the store you'll be linking to. Each store is going to be different, but most stores will have a structure where you can find a pattern. For example, the store you're linking to may have hundreds of products, but each link starts with `http://example.com/products/` and then ends with `product-name/`. If that's the case, we can create a regular expression to create a pattern. Let's take a look at the following steps:

1. From the WordPress admin, go to **Tools | Redirection**.
2. Scroll down to the **Add new redirection** section.
3. In the **Source URL** field, enter this: `/example/([A-Za-z0-9\+\.\-]*)/`.

   The `([A-Za-z0-9\+\.\-]*)` part is a regular expression. It's a bit complicated to explain everything in the regular expression, but what it's basically checking is to see if you've put any combination of numbers, letters, or hyphens in the URL. If you have, then it's a match and now we'll tell you what you can do with the matched text in the URL.

   In the **Target URL** field, enter this: `http://example.com/products/$1/?ref=25`. This URL will take the user to a specific page on example.com. It will take them to /products/$1/, where $1 is what you matched with your regular expression. If your affiliate link looks like `/example/my-first-affiliate-product/`, then the user will be taken to `http://example.com/products/my-first-affiliate-product/?ref=25`. The `?ref=25` part is the special code I've added to the link to let the vendor know who is referring the user. The vendor will give you the special token you have to add to your URLs so they know who referred the user.

4. Check the **Regular expression** checkbox.
5. Click on **Add Redirection**.

You should now have a fully functional regular expression. On your website, you'll be able to enter as many pretty links as you want. The regular expression should make the match and redirect the user to the right page on the vendor's site.

There's more...

Regular expressions are incredibly powerful. You can make all sorts of complex patterns, match different parts of the pattern, and then do something with each of the matched sections.

 A good place to learn more about regular expressions is http://www.regular-expressions.info/.

Regular expressions are pretty complex. If you aren't too comfortable with writing code, you may want to outsource this to a developer. An agency that excels at small jobs like this is **Codeable** (http://codeable.io).

Creating a coupon with restrictions

The coupon system built into WooCommerce isn't simplistic. There are all sorts of limitations you can add on to coupons to make sure that they're only used in the right way. You can create coupons for specific users, coupons that can be used a certain number of times, or coupons that are limited to certain amounts.

We'll be creating a coupon that you can give out at a conference. It can only be used 100 times, it will only be active for a month, and it can only be used on orders over $50. This will make sure that you don't lose money on your promotions but users still get a good deal.

How to do it...

We'll be creating a regular coupon and then tweaking a few extra settings to add the appropriate restrictions. Let's take a look at the following steps:

1. From the WordPress admin, go to **WooCommerce | Coupons**.
2. Click on **Add Coupon**.
3. Enter the code you want in the **Coupon code** field.
4. Enter the discount you want in the **Coupon amount** field.

   We've configured all of the basic settings. Now we need to add the setting to restrict the coupon.

5. Click on the **Usage Restriction** tab and you'll see a ton of settings you can use to restrict how the coupon is used.

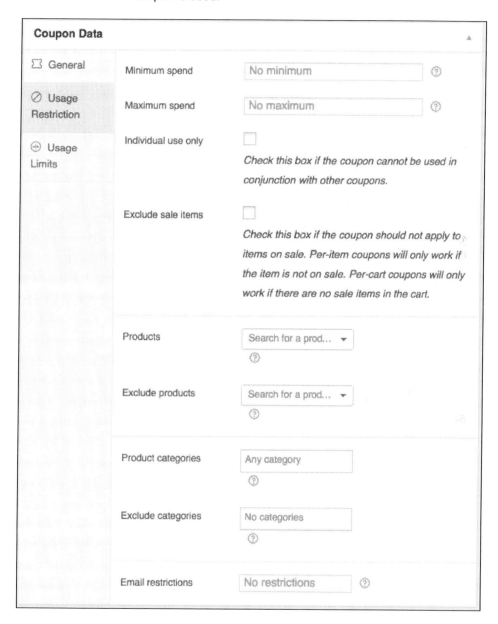

6. Enter 50 into the **Minimum spend** field.
7. You can optionally restrict the coupon to certain products or categories on this tab.

8. Click on the **Usage Limits** tab.

9. Enter `100` into the **Usage limit per coupon** field. This way, only the first 100 people can use the code.

10. Click on the **General** tab.

11. Enter the expiration date in the **Coupon expiry date** field.

12. Click on **Publish**.

There's more...

If you want to bulk-generate coupons, you can use the Smart Coupons extension, which is explained in the next recipe.

Bulk-generating coupons with the Smart Coupons plugin

If you want to create hundreds or thousands of unique coupons, then you probably don't want to do that by hand. You'll want a tool that will let you create a coupon template and use that template to create the unique coupons. That's exactly what WooCommerce Smart Coupons does.

Getting ready

You'll need the WooCommerce Smart Coupons plugin, available at WooThemes.com, installed and activated on your site.

How to do it...

Smart Coupons is primarily meant for bulk coupon generation, so we'll be going straight to that page. Let's take a look at the following steps:

1. From the WordPress admin, go to **WooCommerce | Smart Coupon**.

2. Enter the number of coupons you want to create in the **Number of Coupons to Generate** field.

3. Enter all of the settings you would for a regular coupon; for example, **Discount Type**, **Coupon Amount**, and **Usage limit per coupon**.

4. There are two settings at the bottom of the screen that apply to generating coupons—**Prefix for Coupon Code** and **Suffix for Coupon Code**.

 Prefixes and suffixes are nice for visually grouping coupons. If you create 100 coupons for an event, you can identify that coupon at a glance on the order page if it has a prefix/suffix.

5. Click on **Generate and Add to Store**.

If you go to **WooCommerce | Coupons**, you'll be able to see all of your automatically generated coupons.

There's more...

If you want to manually look at or edit the coupons before creating them, you can tweak the last two settings on the bulk coupon page. They'll allow you to export the generated coupons in a CSV file. You can then reimport them using Smart Coupons through the **Import Coupons** tab on the Smart Coupons page.

Changing the default e-mail's from address

When you create your store, WooCommerce automatically uses the admin e-mail in WordPress as the default from address in e-mails. This is convenient for many users, but, you may want your site admin to only get admin e-mails and for someone else to get responses from customers. This can be done using one of the many WordPress hooks.

How to do it...

We'll need to add a little bit of code to modify the from address, by performing the following steps:

1. Open up your theme's `functions.php` file or a custom WooCommerce plugin.

2. At the bottom of the file, add the following code:

```
add_filter( 'wp_mail_from',
'woocommerce_cookbook_wp_mail_from', 99 );
```

This code tells WordPress that we want to change the standard from address in any e-mails sent. Now we need to actually write the function to do that.

3. Add the following code beneath the preceding code:

```
function woocommerce_cookbook_wp_mail_from() {
    return html_entity_decode( 'yourname@yourstore.com' );
}
```

This function returns an e-mail address in the correct format to replace the default. You can, of course, change `yourname@yourstore.com` to whatever you want.

4. Save and upload the file.

Now, any e-mails you or your customers receive from your website should use that new address.

Sending follow-up e-mails after purchase

Achieving top-of-mind awareness is one really good way to keep your customers coming back. You could do this by sending out newsletters, which I definitely recommend. Newsletters are really good for updates and sharing product information, but they aren't terribly good at getting feedback from users. You could instead send out automated e-mails after someone purchases a product with the Follow Up Emails plugin. You'll stay top-of-mind and you can also get some feedback from the customer.

Getting ready

You need to have the Follow up emails plugin, available at WooThemes.com, installed and activated on your site. You'll also need at least one product on your site.

How to do it...

Follow up emails has its own section in the WordPress admin. We'll have to go through the process of creating a follow-up e-mail and then select how it gets sent out. Let's take a look at the following steps:

1. From the WordPress admin, go to **Follow-Up Emails | New Email**.

   You'll only see a few settings, as **Follow-Up Emails** does everything in a step-by-step process.

2. Enter a name for the e-mail in the **Name your email** field. This name is just for your use, so you don't need to worry about a customer seeing it.

3. Now select the type of e-mail you wish to send. For our purposes, we want to send out an e-mail after a product has been purchased. For that, we want to select **Storewide Email**.

4. Click on **Continue to Step 2**.

5. Enter the subject line in the **What is your subject line** field.

6. Under the **When should the email be sent** field, you should select **Days**. A few more fields will appear. In the empty field before **Days**, enter **7** or however many days you wish to wait before sending the e-mail. In the dropdown after **Days**, select **after first purchase**.

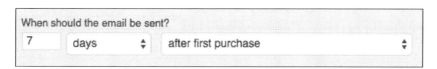

7. You can optionally only send this e-mail for selected products with the **Do you wish to email for** field. For our example, we're just asking the customer how they like the product for every product in the store.

8. Click on **Continue to Step 3**.

9. Now write the e-mail to the customer. You can use some placeholders in the e-mail; these are listed right next to the text editor.

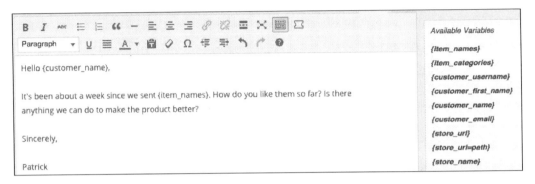

10. Click on **Save your email**.

You'll be redirected to a page that lists all of your e-mails. Make sure that the **Status** is listed as **Active**.

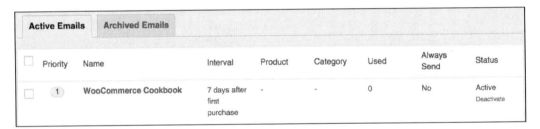

Now, the next time a customer makes a purchase, an e-mail will be queued up and sent out.

There's more...

You can do so much more with the Follow up emails plugin. It's an entire e-mail automation marketing service built into a plugin, so you can use it right from your dashboard. You can send out multiple e-mails per product, per category, based on when users register, and more. One of the more effective strategies is to use Follow up emails to send out coupons several months after their first order. It keeps you top-of-mind and adds an extra incentive to make another order.

Index

Thank you for buying
WooCommerce Cookbook

About Packt Publishing

Packt, pronounced 'packed', published its first book, *Mastering phpMyAdmin for Effective MySQL Management*, in April 2004, and subsequently continued to specialize in publishing highly focused books on specific technologies and solutions.

Our books and publications share the experiences of your fellow IT professionals in adapting and customizing today's systems, applications, and frameworks. Our solution-based books give you the knowledge and power to customize the software and technologies you're using to get the job done. Packt books are more specific and less general than the IT books you have seen in the past. Our unique business model allows us to bring you more focused information, giving you more of what you need to know, and less of what you don't.

Packt is a modern yet unique publishing company that focuses on producing quality, cutting-edge books for communities of developers, administrators, and newbies alike. For more information, please visit our website at www.packtpub.com.

About Packt Open Source

In 2010, Packt launched two new brands, Packt Open Source and Packt Enterprise, in order to continue its focus on specialization. This book is part of the Packt open source brand, home to books published on software built around open source licenses, and offering information to anybody from advanced developers to budding web designers. The Open Source brand also runs Packt's open source Royalty Scheme, by which Packt gives a royalty to each open source project about whose software a book is sold.

Writing for Packt

We welcome all inquiries from people who are interested in authoring. Book proposals should be sent to author@packtpub.com. If your book idea is still at an early stage and you would like to discuss it first before writing a formal book proposal, then please contact us; one of our commissioning editors will get in touch with you.

We're not just looking for published authors; if you have strong technical skills but no writing experience, our experienced editors can help you develop a writing career, or simply get some additional reward for your expertise.

Building E-Commerce Solutions with WooCommerce

ISBN: 978-1-78216-640-5   Paperback: 132 pages

Learn to transform your WordPress website into a fully featured online store

1. Explore this do-it-yourself e-commerce solution using WordPress and WooCommerce.

2. Set up payment and shipping methods.

3. Manage your online store and expand its functions using plugins.

WordPress 3.7 Complete
Third Edition

ISBN: 978-1-78216-240-7   Paperback: 404 pages

Make your first end-to-end website from scratch with WordPress

1. Learn how to build a WordPress site quickly and effectively.

2. Find out how to create content that's optimized to be published on the Web.

3. Learn the basics of working with WordPress themes and playing with widgets.

Please check **www.PacktPub.com** for information on our titles

WordPress Web Application Development

ISBN: 978-1-78328-075-9   Paperback: 376 pages

Develop powerful web applications quickly using cutting-edge WordPress web development techniques

1. Develop powerful web applications rapidly with WordPress.

2. Practical scenario-based approach with ready-to-test source code.

3. Learning how to plan complex web applications from scratch.

WordPress Theme Development Beginner's Guide
Third Edition

ISBN: 978-1-84951-422-4   Paperback: 252 pages

Learn how to design and build great WordPress themes

1. Learn how to design WordPress themes and build them from scratch.

2. Learn how to create a WordPress theme design using HTML5 and CSS3.

3. With clear and easy to follow worked examples to help you build your first WordPress theme if you've never done it before.

Please check **www.PacktPub.com** for information on our titles

19853119R00138

Made in the USA
Lexington, KY
30 November 2018